Writing Handbooks

Freelance Writing for Newspapers

SECOND EDITION

Jill Dick

A & C Black • London

Second edition 1998
First published 1991

A & C Black (Publishers) Limited
35 Bedford Row, London WC1R 4JH

ISBN 0–7136–4737–X

A CIP catalogue record for this book is
available from the British Library

Typeset in 10½ on 12 pt Sabon
Printed and bound in Great Britain by
Creative Print and Design (Wales), Ebbw Vale

Books in the 'Writing Handbooks' series

Other books for writers

Contents

To Jim

standfirst*

Freelance writers are an important factor in producing newspapers. The sense of excitement, of being reborn every week, every day or even several times a day, and of living on a fast-moving platform of people and events makes papers grow and thrive – and the work of freelances, each with a fresh view of the outside world, is invaluable. Freelances don't work in newspaper offices and are not on the payroll of any paper; they just take it upon themselves to submit what they write to editors, hoping they will like it enough to print it and pay for it.

Anyone can be a freelance but dedication to the task is vital. You may get a few ideas today, research into them a little next week and write your piece a month later, and even that unhurried approach will require a degree of discipline if your work is to be publishable. Tighten up the schedule, determining that by a particular date or within a prearranged time you will think, study, research, write, rewrite and rewrite again – however many times it takes before you are satisfied – and a firm plan of action becomes necessary. Do you only wish to write a little now and again when you feel like doing it? There is no 'right' way and no 'wrong' way. In considering the quantity of writing, whatever *you* want is right for you. The quality of what you write, and that alone, will determine how successful you will be.

The advantages of freelancing are many. There is no daily grind of getting to and from an office, nobody restricts your work (staff writers are bound to their employers and are not expected to write for other papers) and you can work when, where and how you wish, writing whatever you want for whichever papers you like without anyone looking over your shoulder and telling you what to do. You'd feel more confident if somebody *were* looking over your shoulder, at least at the beginning?

*An intro separate from the story itself. See page 157 for more newspaper jargon.

1

This book is the answer. Here you will find techniques and working tips that journalists pick up over a lifetime in the job. Discover who does what – and how – in the making of a newspaper, where freelances fit into the editor's plans, and the importance of advertising. Read about the huge range of markets available for freelance copy, find out who owns what, the dominance of the provincial press and where to find the best market guides. Learn about intros, the shape of news, linkage, wimp words, come-ons, cut-offs and many other tricks of the trade.

How will you maintain a flow of usable ideas? What regular columns and corners are waiting to be filled – and how do you fill them? Does grammar matter? What is house style? Letters to the Editor, interviewing, the task of research, taking pictures – these and many other matters are discussed in these pages. There is an important section on the use of computer technology and another about online markets for writers. A chapter about the essential business aspect of writing deals with self-assessment of income tax, keeping records, training, copyright, rates of pay, being paid – and more.

As freelances the whole gamut of writing activities is open to us. We can be reporters dealing largely or exclusively with news, feature writers delving into and developing individual stories at greater depth, reviewers of books, films or theatre, or specialist writers on a wide assortment of topics. Whatever the finished product, it is the result of craftsmanship unobserved by readers. Here you will learn, as thousands of people who write for newspapers have learned, that it is always the ordinary people behind a story that make it live. Without people there would be no news, for to a journalist they are the breath of life. It is also important to understand and recognise our own feelings if we are to express them in words for readers; unless we can do so we won't be able to recognise them in other people.

Notwithstanding the value of precept and tuition, the following attitudes of mind earn more than any particular ability or skill:

- Understand freelancing is a business and your fee is a measure of success
- Offer some speciality (but a product mix is the best recipe for steady work)
- Always be professional and keep an open mind

- Be methodical, persistent and up to date
- Look for the unusual angle and don't scorn small pieces
- Sell to other media – magazines, local radio, regional and local papers
- Be reliable, flexible and respect editors' time
- Establish fees, refundable expenses and deadlines *before* starting work
- Take pictures to enhance your earnings
- Be firm regarding fees without overestimating your worth
- See yourself and your work as part of the newspaper business

One thing this book can't do is teach you to write – no book can do that. It is only by sitting down and *writing* that anyone becomes a writer.

1. Who Does What — and How

On a major national daily it is normal for each separate job in the making of a newspaper to be done by a particular individual who does nothing else. But a small local weekly or a low-circulation freesheet may number its total staff on the fingers of one hand, and in such a case most of them will be able to turn their hands to a variety of tasks.

The system involved in ensuring regular and reliable publishing of newspapers of all sizes and circulations depends on an elaborate but well-practised structure. Everyone working in it must know (and adhere to) the working pattern which is governed by two essentials: a carefully defined administrative responsibility about who does what and the awareness of deadlines.

The production of a newspaper is generally organised into five main departments. The editorial department is no doubt of most concern to readers of this book. The other main departments are administration (the building, secretarial, finance, stationery, etc.), production (composing and printing, including paper and machinery), sales (which includes distribution) and advertising. Of these departments only the last two generate income. Even the sales department often runs at a net loss, having enormous expenses in itself, even with occasional special promotions. What a weight of responsibility rests on advertising!

Newspaper pages are made of headlines, body text, pictures (commonly known as 'pix') and advertisements — and it is the advertisements that are allotted their places first. Discussions between advertising agents and the paper's representatives determine the size, shape and design of the display and classified advertisements. The overall plan for each edition is carefully balanced and often precise pages and positions on them are negotiated and paid for by advertisers. For every edition the advertising department produces what is known as a 'dummy', showing all the pages and which spaces on each have been sold

5

to particular advertisers. It is these dummies that provide a basic framework on which the editor and his team set to work at daily or twice-daily editorial conferences where the planning and progress of the day's edition are checked.

Fewer than half the two hundred or so journalists on the pay-roll of most leading national daily newspapers are likely to be writers. On regional papers an even smaller proportion of the total number of employees spend their time writing and a small weekly, with pages of advertisements and restricted editorial space, will need very few people writing to fill it. Let that be a sober reminder to us all of our real place in the world of newspapers. The most important people? You may be surprised to hear they are the hard-working teams involved in distribution – getting the papers to the places where people can and will buy them. If the finished paper is not available for sale, all the effort and dedication of everyone working on it, including the writers, will count for naught. Nor do we come second in the pecking order. That place goes to the page designers – particularly the front page designers. The paper may be available to buy where people expect to find it, but if it is not immediately visually attractive it will not be bought in sufficient numbers to render the whole enterprise viable.

Only then – in third position of importance – do we writers count. But at least we can take comfort from knowing writers are as essential a part of the huge structured organisational plan as are many other employees in the making of a newspaper.

The editor

A national newspaper editor holds an insecure job although he is like a commander-in-chief of an army. He is the overseer of all departments and is responsible for the whole content as well as for the style and image of the paper. How much he chooses to work at the daily or weekly job himself is often a matter of personal choice; some may have risen to their present positions from a background of reporting or feature writing and enjoy still being part of the writing team as well as its head, preferring to write their own leader columns and be involved with the running of all departments; others prefer to spend their time in meetings, leaving the staff to run the day-to-day business. On smaller papers where staff numbers are lower the editor won't be able to sit in policy-making solitude for long and may happily spend days as busily as any of the staff, turning to any job in the office that needs doing. It's a man-of-all-work editor for the small papers, an editor-in-chief with deputies and assistants for the big ones and usually a mixture of both between the two. If the editor is ill or on holiday, his tasks fall to the deputy editor and assistant editors, if any are appointed, who rank in seniority between the editor and the heads of various departments or sections of the paper. How many of these exist or are appointed will depend on the size, circulation and publication frequency of individual titles.

On the editor's shoulders rests the ultimate responsibility for the paper's content and its production. If anything it carries causes any legal trouble he is the one to go to jail, and if it's late coming out he has to accept the blame regardless of what caused the delay and whoever else might have been more directly responsible. Speed is everything, for a newspaper's life is short – at the most a fortnight, sometimes a week, perhaps only a day and often just a few hours. Failing to meet production deadlines is dire; the penalty for delay will be a day's work lost, possibly another little nail being polished to hold down the lid of the paper's coffin – and perhaps even the editor's head.

What the editor has to decide

In the day-to-day work pattern, the editor has to decide how to fill the space allotted to him for each edition with text, headlines and pictures. The first tasks in the preparation of a particular edition involve a lot of preplanning. Sales folk on the telephone and out around the area will have sold space for display and classified advertisements, and the spaces for them will already have been allocated, as they always go in first. Specialist columns will have been set up or put on the planning menu from decisions made the day before or even two days earlier, and there will be similar matters to settle regarding editions for tomorrow or several days ahead as well as the urgent decisions to be made about the next immediate edition.

The space to be allocated to feature material is determined according to the paper's size and the amount of space given over to advertisements and news. The former bring in revenue, the latter has to be paid for. Features also cost money (not enough, in the opinion of many freelances) but they are exclusive and valuable to the paper. A leader writer will have had talks with the editor (who may choose to write the leader himself) and decisions will have been made about the topic of the lead, its width and length. Regular pieces like television pages (if not in a separate section which is dealt with by its own team), the weather forecast and the crossword puzzle, for instance, will have been given their places and the only spaces left will be reserved for the 'hard' news that will surely come in all day long.

On the home news front, local and smaller papers serving a defined circulation area get their up-to-date news by doing the 'calls' – just asking around. Other news stories will originate from readers phoning in with tip-offs about interesting pieces of news that might be worth following up. Press releases about forthcoming events already in the pipeline and about new matters pour into newspaper offices, and some will carry the germ of a story sufficiently interesting for a reporter to investigate.

For the leading papers, the most valuable providers of news are the agencies set up in many other countries to gather news from all over the world and transmit it quickly and reliably to anyone who wants it. Modern technology has had a profound effect on the methods of distributing news; some 10 million words *per day* are received by various newspapers in London 'on the wire'.

To the editor also falls the task of making the paper attractive while keeping it as regular readers like it. They prefer layout they feel comfortable with (as do customers in oft-visited supermarkets), know their papers by the 'look' of the type and often raise an outcry when it changes. Balancing readers' dislike of change with the need for a bright attractive appearance is just one of the editor's problems.

The appearance of regular parts of the paper is carefully planned. Papers are either tabloid (usually 7 columns wide) or broadsheet (usually 8 or 9 columns). Different sections of the paper are made instantly recognisable by their distinctive typefaces and layout formats. So a headline for a gripping news item will use a different typeface from one over a piece quoting stock market prices, and lists such as radio or television programmes are given individual and easily read typefaces.

The editor decides (or his team decides with his approval) where features and news will sit on the pages or sections of pages allotted to them. If your accepted feature, for instance, gets a 'good' place on the page (that's traditionally a little right of centre on the top half of a right-hand page, a spot to which, experts tell us, the eye is most naturally drawn) you can be reasonably confident it was considered important enough to hold that place. That doesn't mean, of course, that other spots in the paper are not important but, given the time and opportunity afforded by computer usage for easy movement of whole stories on the page-layout screen, pages are now often designed to please the eye rather than to satisfy editorial demands. The practice developed a long time ago (and obtains on some papers to this day) that a story anywhere on the front page 'above the line', i.e. above the halfway fold where the bottom half of the paper might not be visible in a newsagent's rack or on his counter, presented such a great sales factor that it should attract a higher rate of pay than the same story would in a less valued position. The truth is that every story in the paper is valuable for that day's issue or it wouldn't be there. Everything in this cut-throat world of competition is costed most carefully and each story, each picture, each word must earn its place.

As for the news, that comes in all the time. It's not all stuff that will make readers gasp or even be mildly surprised, for in this news category must come 'news' that is already expected. A local paper might be waiting for a statement from a hospital, for instance, following a serious fire in a hotel in which several people have been injured; a regional evening paper would hope to catch the verdict from a particular trial; and a national paper must get the result of a big football match or a report of a major race meeting. Much of the news is not unexpected but is not actually to hand at the early planning stage. One way and another, through avenues well-established and just occasionally by unexpected routes, the news comes in and eventually takes its place in the day's layout.

The editor's team – including freelances

On national dailies and Sunday papers (and on some regional papers) the night editor heads his own team and is almost as important as the editor. National and regional morning papers go to press at about 3 am, and the hours leading up to that time are every bit as busy, albeit in a different way, as those of daylight.

As strictly speaking all editorial content, i.e. non-advertising, is either news or features, there is one news editor and one features editor. The latter holds a most important job and his duties include briefing freelances, discussing work with them, checking copy and seeing payment matters are passed on to the accounts department. More freelance feature material comes into the average newspaper than any other sort of freelance copy. Indeed, when most freelance writers think of writing for newspapers they automatically think of features.

Newspapers must always be up to date and although features are not news they must be timely in that they must relate to something that is in the news. Time and season are inescapable concepts to bear in mind for all feature material, and everything must be hung on 'pegs' of current news. Sections of a paper involving the features editor might cover Letters to the Editor, horoscopes, in-depth investigative features, holidays, the diary column, cookery, fashion, health, gardening, children's interests, the home, showbiz, crosswords, interviews and the gossip column. He might also have to deal with other topics such as motoring that (on some papers) may be the province of specialist writers.

It pays to remember that the larger a newspaper the more it can afford to employ specialists to write on individual topics such as music and live theatre. These writers will often be free-lances who have gained a 'standby' place among the paper's contacts by having previously impressed the editor or features editor with their expertise and ability. Study of your own paper will reveal regularly published columns or that the same correspondent is on hand with an authoritative view on aircraft construction, for example, at the time of any major air disaster. Wise beginners will naturally avoid these topics and spot ones that do not feature regularly.

All writing for newspapers demands timeliness and a point of view. A feature carries facts and figures generally brought in to support a particular train of thought or a special point, but its main *raison d'être* is to explain, elucidate and expand before reaching a conclusion. It is not a disclosure of previously unknown facts (news) but an inevitably biased argument on a particular point. Feature writers give papers flavour and originality. Their words give copy rhythm and colour in the most appropriate style for the market. Top feature writers will be highly regarded – and paid.

Such is the pressure of work on a big daily that there will be city, political and foreign editors. At the time of writing all nationals except the *Financial Times* also employ a specialist sports editor. Where there is a separate section devoted to a specific topic within the features editor's aegis, it will probably boast its own editor (and maybe even assistants) as well as staff writers and reporters attached for varying periods. Leading papers will also employ regular and occasional overseas correspondents, almost certainly based in key cities round the world, who will always be prepared to fly to 'flash points' within their reach when required.

Specialist work such as parliamentary or investigative reporting is not likely to be the province of the freelance. Political and parliamentary correspondents are highly skilled and experienced writers who spend most of their time at Westminster. The job of these correspondents is to report on parliamentary debates and affairs and to write notes and sketches. Meanwhile lobby correspondents are busy sounding out what's going on behind the scenes, writing background reports and trying to interpret government actions and ideas. Their task is to receive information provided by government spokesmen, but you'll seldom get them to admit what's going on for it's usually off the record. Every time you read 'Rumours in Whitehall suggest . . .' you'll know they're there.

The news editor looks after all incoming news, while the foreign editor (if there is one appointed) selects and works on all stories coming in from overseas and is responsible for the work of foreign correspondents. All the news from whatever source, on whatever topic and whenever it arrives is balanced with feature material, perhaps already placed, and changes of positioning and rearrangements of copy are commonplace.

Reporters are the hard-working folk at the root of a paper's activities. They are likely to be out and about collecting information from tip-offs supplied by the office, waiting to file the latest news on a 'running' story or they might be carrying out any one of a dozen duties in the circulation area. It's considered to be the foot of the ladder in the newspaper world but it's the place where many a leading journalist began learning the craft. A reporter or a local corespondent carries considerable responsibility. He (or she) may be fresh out of training school or an older more experienced writer who doesn't want to change his job; regardless of age, on papers covering a wide geographical area he's probably overworked as well.

Weeklies, especially in country districts, cannot hope to find out what is happening in every town and village every week, and many events will go unreported (to the dissatisfaction of readers) unless somebody takes care of the community. It's a challenging job and one that should not be undertaken without careful consideration. Being committed to maintaining a flow of news from a small town or village or district can be a chore when the reporter wants to go on holiday or is ill. Weekly reporters may not be paid, preferring to be volunteers for the job, or they may receive only a small remuneration – but the first rule of the job is never to let the community down.

Doing the 'calls' is also a regular task. This means calling on the people or organisations likely to know what's going on: the police and fire stations, local hospitals, the Town Hall, the Citizens' Advice Bureau, the morgue, the courts, schools, health clinics, community centres – anywhere and everywhere in the locality where a spokesman is able and willing to impart news or the basis of a news story to pass on to readers of the paper. How often a reporter does the calls will depend on how often the paper is published, but once a good network of contacts is established they will make contact with the paper themselves when they have anything to report. As a welcome by-product, reporting skills benefit out of all proportion to the apparently humdrum level of the job. Making quick decisions about copy, learning how to present it clearly in print and over the phone, developing legible handwriting, an increasing awareness about what is and what is not newsworthy, and a growing confidence make this a worthwhile job for a freelance at any stage. Also, for countless readers the local reporter is the only 'real' journalist they see or ever will see, so on him (or her) will their opinion of the newspaper depend. Illogical and slightly daunting this may be, but it is an extra reason for a freelance to do the job well and gain great satisfaction from it.

There are generally two editorial conferences during the course of an edition's preparation, and the business of the day is not complete until the sub-editors have finished their tasks. Much has been written about the work of sub-editors – and not all of it presents them in a flattering light. 'They are just peasants who only want to ruin our precious copy,' swear some writers, both staff and freelance, and there is no doubt that sometimes what appears in print doesn't sit happily with what the writer wanted or hoped for. But much of the misunderstanding is due to ignorance: not only on the part of the sub-editors (although it is sometimes so) but also on the part of the writer. Few freelances have the chance to see subs, as they are called, at work and to know – let alone understand – the difficulties they face. Phrases like 'repeats himself again and again', 'come to a complete halt' and 'every single day' do not, as some writers imagine, make a sub feel he is worth his salary; more probably he sighs as he reaches for his deleting pencil and scores through the redundant adjectives and adverbs. Will writers never learn? As someone who has been a staff writer, a sub-editor and a freelance journalist, I can see faults on all sides. Life on the sub's table of a major regional evening paper on Budget Day, with a Chancellor of the Exchequer being agonisingly slow to reveal the nitty-gritty everyone wants to know, is not an experience for the faint-hearted and I am quite surprised to have lived through such torment.

Sub-editors, those most important people, have the job of ensuring all staff-written and freelance copy is ready to be printed. The chief subs and their teams (which may be separate for individual sections of a large paper) exert a great impact on how the paper will look when it is finished for their tasks include checking facts, correcting grammar and punctuation to conform to the house style (see page 70), writing crossheads (see page 113) and headlines with setting instructions (headlines sell papers, especially on Sundays, more than the contents or even what's on the rest of the front page), and inserting full information about the size, shape and typography of each story.

Typography is a fascinating subject, and the ability to select the right typeface and use it to best effect is a most valuable skill. The typographer is to the text as the producer is to a play or a film. Type is measured in points, a point being 0.01383 of an inch, which gives approximately 72 points to the inch. This refers to the depth of the body of metal on which a letter stands, not to the actual size of the letter. Because there are small bevels at the top and bottom of the little metal block, the actual face size is always less than the body size. To establish a working norm it is accepted in the printing world that the point size equals the total size of the lower-case alphabet. This is measured from the top of the highest 'ascender' (d, for instance) to the bottom of the lowest 'descender' (like q).

The work of the subs is not easy. It will vary according to the size of a paper and its frequency of publication, but consider how you would interpret the job specification: to shape the material in the form of presentation decided by the chief sub so as to bring out the point of a story, to condense it more effect-

13

ively than can be done by cutting, and to make it more readable. A sub must have a sound knowledge of the laws of libel and contempt, of central and local government organisation, of the various types of court and the pitfalls to be avoided when reporting from them, of newspaper terms, of the organisation for which he works and of the paper's edition times, with deadlines for copy, pix and pages. Added to this a sub-editor must ensure the copy is in good taste and good English while observing the writer's own concept and the needs of the reader.

Subs cope with copy from reporters, news agencies, public relations and publicity sources, prepare the text with all the acknowledged methods of marking, advise layout subs about lengths of stories and page layouts, perhaps write revised stories to include later material on those already running, handle pictures, and maybe act as copy-tasters as well, selecting stories for special importance, human interest and entertainment value. They must be ready to deal with copy arriving often in quantity and certainly with increasing speed and urgency as the paper's deadline approaches . . . and through it all they must keep calm and practical. Quite an exacting job, isn't it? As a great deal of a paper's success depends on how it looks, sales being in known relation to appearance rather than news content, the best tabloid headline and layout subs are highly paid.

Eventually page layouts are prepared so the compositors have an exact guide to the appearance of each page when it's made up. On national papers the front page is generally the last to be 'put to bed', in order to maintain topicality until the very last moment (remember the importance of an attractive front page). When the editor is satisfied everything is in order, it's time for the many skilled people who have been handling the current edition to hand it over.

Putting it away

Few developments have changed modern life so rapidly as the advance of technology. In the world of newspapers it is likened to a second industrial revolution, even greater in its effects than the invention and widespread introduction of the Caxton printing press. Nor is the new world only in the actual printing, for computer typesetting and on-screen make-up have brought enormous changes – not without attendant problems of another sort, as some would hasten to remind me.

Older journalists recall the excitement of the first days of the new order, which seemed little short of a miracle of design and ingenuity, when photo-typesetting replaced 'hot' metal and the (literally) revolutionary rotary press saw the beginning of the end of the old hand-set flatbed printing. This printing method involves plates full of text set into cylinders and enormous rolls of newsprint. The inked plates are forced on to the paper which is printed on both sides at incredible speed before being cut, folded and stacked to the required finish.

A decade ago came electronic layout and design via the use of desktop computers in the office environment which allow the easy make-up of pages of text and pix on screen. Copy is not written on paper in the office, for there isn't any at this stage, but by 'direct input' (sometimes called 'direct entry'). Anyone familiar with a word-processor will have first-hand experience of the same system on a personal level. With the copy on-screen in front of them, journalists can delete errors, insert sentences, move whole paragraphs and blocks or import them from elsewhere, all at the touch of a keyboard. Completed pages are then photographed and set in the negative to be fused onto polymer sheets for web-offset litho or letterpress printing. Goodbye to old composing rooms – and to the old-style compositors. What would earlier printers and writers think if they could see a national newspaper in production today?

Nor does the miracle end there. If, for instance, the editorial and advertising preparation is done in one place but the actual printing takes place elsewhere, perhaps in several widely separated print units in other parts of the UK or even of the world, the technological marvel of facsimile transmission takes over. It is now as quick and easy to print the paper in a different country as in the UK; the *Financial Times* prints its European edition in Frankfurt, while the *International Guardian* prints in Marseilles. There is already plenty to marvel at in today's 'electronic' newspapers and the experts tell us there is plenty more ahead.

Advertisers

When it comes to the business of who does which job in putting a newspaper together, the advertising folk take priority. Advertisements are always positioned before anything else and there are several reasons why this is so. The prime one is the business reality that advertisers are paying the paper, i.e. buying the space their advertisements occupy. Although many newspaper proprietors would have you believe their pages hold advertisements for more altruistic reasons, there is no doubt the money received from advertisers, especially the big regular spenders, is the life blood of newspapers. It is not unusual for a serious Sunday newspaper to reserve 60 per cent of the whole paper for advertisements and to carry as many as 150 display and over 4,000 classified ads in a single edition. The total income to newspapers is colossal: in 1995 the nationals sold advertising space to the value of £1,336,000, while local papers did even better with a revenue of £1,871,000.

But the true value of advertising can be assessed only in the context of other considerations. The wider the spread of papers, the more outlets there are for an advertiser's message and the stronger becomes his bargaining power (although his feedback from readers is more difficult to record). Advertisers know, too, that they are even more easily blown about by the fortunes of the times than are newspapers themselves. The country's overall economic position will give an indication of the current health of the newspaper business; is a recession round the corner, are interest rates high, is unemployment rising? Matters way outside the newspaper world can have an inevitable (and sometimes devastating) effect on it. They will affect all papers (yes, your local weekly as well) to a greater or lesser degree depending on how much they rely on selling their advertising space.

British newspapers are not subsidised (except by being zero-rated for Value Added Tax). If they didn't accept advertising their cover prices would be higher, sales would be lower and many would go out of business. So their income depends on two sources, advertising revenue and sales; in what proportion will depend on several factors. In some cases there may be special influences at work as well; the speedy collapse of Communism in much of Eastern Europe at the end of the 1980s, for instance, dealt a severe blow to the *Morning Star*. When the Soviet Union cut its order by 6,000 copies a day, pagination was reduced from 12 to 8 pages, the editorial staff was cut from 40 to 28, and the paper faced an annual £400,000 loss of income. Advertising space is not likely to sell well in a paper experiencing such troubled times. And if advertisers don't support the paper . . .

The popular papers have less need to rely on advertising revenue than have their more serious competitors, and regional papers have a higher proportion of direct, i.e. non-agency, advertising. Almost 90 per cent of advertising comes from agencies which employ people to do the vital work of researching the potential profitability of placing advertisements and to buy the advertising space. The agencies depend for their fees on the success of their work, i.e. readership response to the ads they place, which is carefully monitored. If the agencies don't get it right they, as well as their customers, will suffer because next time the advertisers will use another agency. So a good agency, keen to satisfy and retain the folk who pay their bills, will have done a great deal of professional research and taken pains to ensure their advertisements are put before the eyes of readers with particular proclivities and lifestyles. In advertising, jobs, property and cars are the big earners, and premium rates often apply to advertising spaces on the front page, the first right-hand page (to which a reader's eyes are naturally drawn on opening the paper), and the first motoring advertisement in any particular issue.

Advertising agencies swear by readership surveys, particularly the National Readership Surveys which categorise readers in the following age groups: 15–24, 25–34, 35–44, 45–54, 55–64 and over 65. Tough competition means agencies have their facts and figures coldly cut and dried, and work on a clear idea of where we all fit into today's society. They've assessed what sort of people the readers of any particular newspaper will be and the advertisements they place will reflect that estimated socio-economic class. They fully realise not all readers fall into the same group in every respect; there will always be left-wing supporters reading traditional right-wing papers, and die-hard traditionalists liking the *News of the World*, so the best even advertising agencies can do is aim at a general assessment of readership.

The freesheets are most dependent on selling advertising space; it is their sole source of income and few can survive for long with falling revenue and a pessimistic economic prognosis. But their very vulnerability is also their strength; they can target readership more accurately and they may respond to revenue difficulties more rapidly and with greater versatility than paid-for local weeklies in the same areas. Training, design, improved distribution and better quality in editorial matter are seen as the key factors in keeping the free papers vigorous and in good health.

Is there any limit to how far a paper will go to attract business and how much an advertiser will pay? On 11 February 1996 the telecommunications giant Mercury bought every display advertising space in the *Sunday Times* to push its business telecommunications campaign. A few weeks later the *Daily Mirror* turned itself into a bluish-coloured advertisement for the day as part of a Pepsi-Cola campaign to convert its label from red to 'an exciting new shade of blue'. Some senior journalists were outraged. 'To devote half the front page and two inside pages to the marketing of a soft drink,' complained Roy Greenslade, the paper's former editor, 'was a disgraceful exercise.' On 24 August 1995 *The Times* was free – given away to anyone who wanted a copy in a half-million-pound promotion to mark the launch of Microsoft Windows 95 software. Not all journalists were happy at making the paper a giant advertising sheet for Microsoft. (Perhaps they couldn't get past the thought that if Bill Gates, owner and developer of the company, dropped a $100 bill in the street it would cost him more to pick it up than it would to leave it where it fell: just five seconds of his time is worth well over $100.)

That's the way with newspapers. Love 'em or hate 'em, they're never dull. They can't afford to be. Enterprising promotional schemes have a colourful history. The *Daily Herald* in 1933 offered its readers a 16-volume set of the work of Charles Dickens for 11 shillings plus *Herald* coupons. The *Daily Mail*, *Daily Express* and the *News Chronicle* immediately responded by offering similar sets for 10 shillings. A total 11 million of these sets were sold – and a great many extra papers were bought . . .

Notwithstanding the power of advertising, there are strictly controlled parameters to which agencies and newspapers must adhere. The Advertising Standards Authority (2 Torrington Place, London WC1E 7HW *tel* 0171-580 5555 *fax* 0171-631 3051), itself funded by a levy on display advertisements, exists to promote and enforce high standards in all non-broadcast advertisements. Empowered to act independently of both government and the newspaper industry, the Authority aims to ensure advertisements are legal, decent, honest and truthful. And when these high standards are flouted in the case of mail order, dissatisfied customers may obtain redress with the help of the National Newspaper Mail Order Protection Scheme (MOPS) (16 Tooks Court, London EC4A 1LB *tel* 0171-405 6806 *fax* 0171-404 0106).

Watchdogs

All the major papers now have their own ombudsmen whose job is to cope with complaints from the public. As you may guess, ombudsmen are people of considerable experience in journalism and – like ombudsmen in other fields – they need considerable reserves of patience and understanding. Their appointments are part of a new Code of Conduct signed by almost all national papers, but the establishment of ombudsmen isn't without its critics. The fact that ombudsmen are appointed by editors barely suggests impartiality, say the objectors to the scheme. It's almost a case of 'Who takes care of the caretaker's daughter when the caretaker's busy taking care?' and it is hard to see that editors can easily disregard their undoubted conflict of interests when wearing their omsbudmanorial hats.

There is seldom a shortage of complaints being lobbied against the press and they come in all guises from complainants large and small, both public and private. Complaints about the contents of newspapers and the way they behave are dealt with by the Press Complaints Commission (1 Salisbury Square, London EC4 8AE *tel* 0171-353 1248 *fax* 0171-353 8355) but occasionally writers, particularly freelances, find the code of fair play on their side. One such occurrence concerned an advertiser trying to get rich from dishonest dealing with honest, if naive, writers. In 1996 the Morris School of Journalism, which repeatedly offered what it called 'press cards' to buyers of its tutorial material, was found guilty by the Advertising Standards Authority of using misleading promotion for its services. There was considerable anxiety about the school's claim of accreditation to the 'International News Syndicate' – an unknown organisation – before Surrey Trading Standards Department stepped in with an official complaint. It is easy for anyone to make what appear to be 'genuine' press cards: a Hampshire company calling itself Scope International offered prospective buyers what were described as 'genuine accredited press passes to open many doors and provide many advantages'. Buyers ('Save money and be treated like a VIP!') were also offered windscreen stickers ('Why pay for parking?') and business cards 'recognised by local and international police forces and most authorities worldwide'. For these and associated goodies buyers paid £400 for two years, £600 for five years or £1,000 for life ownership.

On an official level violations against the law are dealt with severely. In December 1995 Richard Stott, the editor of *Today* newspaper, and the newspaper itself were fined £75,000 for contempt after publishing extracts from a book which had been subject to a High Court injunction five months earlier. The book was highly controversial, being about the one-time housekeeper of the Prince of Wales – whose turbulent personal life was rarely out of the headlines and was guaranteed to sell newspapers.

At about the same time the chairman of the Press Complaints Commission proposed safeguards to curb chequebook journalism, in response to public and private concern about five-figure sums paid to witnesses in the trial of Rosemary West – after the dramatic Gloucester murder case had filled more column inches of newsprint than any other such crime in decades.

Most complaints against the press go unrecorded and have no satisfactory result. Among these are the uncounted charges made by writers to almost every paper at one time or another that their copy has been taken without acknowledgement or reward and used by someone else (see page 156). Nor is this 'lifting' as it's euphemistically called (stealing is the word I prefer) confined to little provincial papers where the lifters hope nobody's going to notice. Weeklies who don't mind lifting from other sources know the stories they're likely to be covering or might think of covering will be featured in the regional dailies or evening papers also covering their areas; work that has been researched and written up by those who have already published is sometimes at risk. Lazy editors find using the bones of someone else's story (sometimes with the flesh still attached) is much less work than getting it for themselves. The popular dailies are big offenders, and they're not fussy where they lift from; stories in overseas publications sent in from news agencies or mentioned on radio and television are rich 'source' material just waiting to be given a new byline. Almost any name will do, and the writer credited with having written the story may not even be a real person; use a phantom reporter, goes the twisted logic, and you won't be getting a real one into trouble if there is any.

Baddies exist in every field and it's a pity the sourness they cause can bring the whole industry into disrepute – and cause writers so much anguish. Many ingenious (and sometimes hilarious) ways of stopping idea-stealing have been suggested, but as yet nobody has produced one that is foolproof. One I

20

heard of recently is that ideas should not be submitted directly to newspapers until they have been logged into an 'ideas clearing house' set up and run by an independent third party, a sort of ideasbudsman. I suppose. Hmm . . .

The NUJ (see page 105) publishes an official Code of Conduct for its members. It is accepted among a wide spread of journalists and writers in many fields as a fair and sound guide to how we, staff and freelances alike, should behave in the course of our work. These are its tenets we should observe and support:

1 The highest professional and ethical standards
2 The defence of press freedom
3 Fair and accurate reporting
4 The rights of reply and correction
5 The use of straightforward means to obtain information
6 The avoidance of intrusion into private grief and distress
7 The protection of sources
8 A refusal to accept bribes or to allow other inducements to influence the performance of professional duties
9 There shall be no distortion because of advertising
10 There shall be no discrimination against minorities or social groups
11 There shall be no private advantage from information gained in the course of work
12 There shall be no endorsement of commercial products

Years ago the advent of television was thought by some to herald the death of newspapers. In fact they are far from dying out: the vast amount of paper used as newsprint has varied little over the past seventy-five years. If you made a roll 30 inches wide and wound it round the globe 30,000 times you might have enough to supply all the newspapers printed in the United Kingdom in a single year. Newspapers are alive and kicking, and the changes in the way they're put together have proceeded at a great rate.

The more you get to know about newspaper production and who does what among the people working in it, the more of a marvel it is revealed to be. And every time it's done and the paper is ultimately printed, it all has to be done again, perhaps the very next day. Indeed, a miracle of expertise, enterprise and technology awaits readers for just a few pence.

2. Marketing

Despite wide social changes and the arrival of television, the circulation of newspapers in the UK has altered little in the past forty years. The rise in the cost of newsprint coupled with fierce competition cut the 1990 total circulation figure of nearly 15 million per day to less than 14 million in the first half of 1996, a minimal loss on such a large figure in a period of six years. But it has not all been good news for the press itself. Among its own obituaries in recent years have been those for *Today*, the first daily newspaper to introduce colour in its pages, born March 1986 and died November 1995, *The Correspondent* (September 1989–November 1990), *London Daily News* (February–June 1987) and the *News on Sunday* which enjoyed a brief life in 1987.

As I write there are 10 national dailies, 9 Sunday papers and almost 100 regional dailies; together they have a total annual circulation of about 25 million copies. And what a size some of them are! Just one Sunday edition of a typical broadsheet can carry more information than an educated person three hundred years ago might have read in a lifetime. All national papers, like provincial and local papers, are in private ownership, which means there is no direct government control or restraint, and virtually all are financially independent from any political masters.

It is estimated that 17 per cent of the world's population speak and read English and that 58 per cent of Britons over the age of 16 read a national daily, with about 70 per cent reading a paper on Sundays. Not, of course, that every reader buys a copy: national dailies average 3.2 readers per copy, Sunday papers 2.9 readers per copy and on average 4 people read each copy of every weekly paper sold. There are also thought to be about 500 free papers. (It is difficult to be sure exactly how many free papers there are as they come and go at speed.) The majority get all their income from advertising, and the oldest, incidentally, was launched in the first decade of this century. No government subsidies support commercial papers and there is no tax concession (at the time of writing) apart from the exemption from Value Added Tax on sales. With the cover price often paying for only a small proportion of the huge costs involved in publishing newspapers, the rest is all paid for by advertising. Readers pay the cover prices, but advertisers pay the enormous annual bill of over £6 billion.

Who are the readers?

So who are all these readers? To study them is an essential part of marketing; indeed, the most essential part. How much do we know about them and how much do we need to know? How much do they earn, what are their jobs, what are their future prospects, what do they spend their money on, where do they go for holidays? Advertising pundits know the answers and we can profit from their experience and know-how. Advertising and sales techniques used by commercial television at its launch in 1955 were eye-openers to newspapers. They didn't roll over and die as some gloomy forecasters predicted. They took to heart new ideas and gave the newspaper industry a much-needed shot in the arm. Nowadays there is readership analysis in complex detail, mainly conducted by the National Readership Surveys, a limited company set up on behalf of the newspaper, magazine and advertising industries. Random but highly controlled sampling is taken from the electoral roll. All questions relate to the chief wage-earner or the head of the household. This nth name principle is said to result in more accurate sampling than any other. Against this background, readers are categorised as follows:

A	Upper middle class: higher managerial, administrative or professional	3%
B	Middle class: intermediate managerial, administrative or professional	15%
C1	Lower middle class: supervisory or clerical, and junior managerial, administrative or professional	24.7%
C2	Skilled working class: skilled manual	27.1%
D	Working class: semi-skilled and unskilled manual	17.3%
E	Unclassified, i.e. below any classification level, state pensioners or widows, casual or lowest grade workers and unemployed	12.9%

Per head of population we read a larger number of newspapers than any other country in the world. How we manage to do so is partly luck, in that we are small enough to allow all our national newspapers to be distributed around Britain on a single day. But also, more importantly, we have a great assortment of newspapers in healthy competition with each other, and that ensures there is something to satisfy everyone. The provincial press vastly overshadows the nationals, and local papers are rooted in the population's affections. There's never any shortage of newspapers to read – or to write for.

Looking further afield

We writers are not confined to UK markets, for the rest of the world is open to any freelance who can write what is wanted. Despite the development of cinema early in the 20th century, of radio broadcasting in the 1920s, and of television in the 1940s, newspapers remain a major source of information. In the United States, for example, almost 2,000 daily newspapers print a total of 80 million copies, and almost every copy is read by at least two people. Some 7,500 weekly newspapers are also published, with a combined circulation of approximately 50 million. America's highest-circulation general interest newspaper is *USA Today* with a daily circulation of about 1.5 million copies nationwide, closely followed by the New York *Daily News,* a metropolitan tabloid selling more than 1.3 million copies a day. But when you come to sell across the Atlantic, don't forget that distribution costs and conditions are very different from those prevailing here. Notwithstanding the high sales figures of the few nationwide US papers, not many others have circulations of over 100,000, and the average paper sells only some 50,000 copies a day. Newspaper publishers in the United States estimate that 8 out of 10 adult Americans read a newspaper every day – and the picture is similar in many developed nations.

Take a broad look at newspapers' attitudes and aims – if you could, with so many thousands to consider – and you would find them almost as varied as the people who read them. News, background stories and interesting items may be their staple fare, but there is a fascinating extra dimension about newspapers. They are not just inky words and pictures printed on greyish-white paper; in a sense all their own, newspapers are alive. In their pages you can expect to read about the events of the day, covering anything and everything from changes at a local factory and a fire in a city library to the illness of an international footballer, the financial crisis of an orchestral company and the latest gyrations of international personalities; all is grist to the mill. Writers, appreciating that not all appears directly before the eyes, know only a careful study of the pages of newspapers will reveal their innate social and/or political slant and particular views in general or on a current topic. This is the market study between the lines, one might say, and just as one meeting with a new acquaintance will not reveal his whole character, so newspapers need to be studied thoroughly over a period of time, with an awareness of what to look for, if they are to be understood.

Local and national

A local weekly paper is a good starting point and for many people this will be where the early successes are scored. Never belittle your own work when you sell to these markets and to 'free' papers; the word 'provincial' has no place here when wearing its condescending hat. Weeklies are as important a part of the whole business as any of their mass-circulation daily and regional cousins. Local papers usually stay around longer too, and the contributor whose work can survive repeated study by what is often a personally involved and intensely critical readership is doing very well indeed.

'I could never write for a national paper!' you may be protesting. But a good deal of their daily content is written by ordinary men and women who didn't even think of themselves as writers until they saw their first submissions in print. They write to the papers simply because they have something to say; to let others share their griefs, or their laughs or something that has made a good or bad impact on their lives. One woman wrote an account for the *News of the World* of how her family came to care for the neighbours they were once at war with (and even took to court over their differences). Another writer, whose poor eyesight meant he could only hold down a low-paid job, put almost every penny he earned into taking youngsters from a local children's home on day trips to the sea. Study the 'ordinary' stories told by 'ordinary' folk and you'll soon realise (if you didn't already know) that there is a huge depth of warm-hearted humanity that doesn't make the front pages and is often obscured by the constant daily dirge of evil, death and destruction man everywhere wreaks on his fellow man. Thousands of 'good' stories are just waiting to be told – and when they are, they touch many hearts.

The *Guardian* published a middle-aged widow's reaction when unthinking comforters said, 'What a good thing you've got another,' after her elder daughter was killed in a road accident; a handicapped writer is thrilled to see her recipes printed in a leading daily; writing for weekend colour supplements is no longer a novelty for a hard-working freelance who has learned how to be a thorough professional without going near a training school for journalists. You can never be certain what may be published or where.

Where to sell

The following brief survey of markets (the topic could fill this and several more books if I let it) starts with the national papers, not with any mistaken idea of their superiority but because it has to begin somewhere. My admiration of the enthusiasm, pace and stamina that sustain them approaches awe when extended to the far wider sphere of the hard-working provincial press.

National papers are referred to either as 'qualities' or as 'tabloids' (originally because of their paper size). The qualities are physically larger than the tabloids and are printed on paper of a size known as broadsheet. The term 'heavies' is seldom heard these days in describing the quality papers, although Sunday delivery boys might find it appropriate when weighed down with all the supplements and colour magazines weekend qualities now include in their cover prices. The *Sunday Times* alone weighs about two pounds and 55 per cent of all newspapers are home delivered; after all the big business and high technology that goes into producing them, the last vital task of getting them into the hands of readers is left to an army of schoolchildren working for pocket money. It occurs to me, by the way, that a hole exists in modern technological thinking when hugely expensive and complex machinery bands together all the sections of heavy Sunday papers, for instance, so a buyer has them all contained in a single package, only to have newsagents all over the country rising before dawn a few hours later to split them into their constituent parts simply because the packaged papers won't go through customers' letterboxes. Anyone care to redesign the traditional letterbox?

The quality papers take a serious view of the news, supporting it with informed analysis and comment on political, economic, social and world events, news and comment being kept firmly apart. The arts, business, entertainment, sport, finance, women's affairs, employment and leisure pages feature in all; most of the material for these pages is provided by staff writers, but there is always room for a good freelance who has done a properly researched and well-written job. Motoring, opera, bridge, tapestry – are these your special subjects? They and many others have provided a first success for freelances who feared they'd never find a way in.

Leader pages may reveal a paper's editorial policy, and most have periods of giving particular attention to special groups of readers and their requirements: women (sometimes of a selected age and income group), sports enthusiasts, followers of a current political cause, and classes of readers chosen for topical or other reasons may be targeted by a newspaper for attention – and such deliberate policies will change from time to time. This is but one reason why we can support so many newspapers at once and why careful study of them is essential for the would-be contributor. Nothing replaces personal market study, for each potential writer may have something individual to contribute.

Sunday qualities follow much the same style and most publish several sections and/or colour magazines, the notion being that at the weekends the nation has more time for serious consideration of the state of the world, with leisure topics taking a prominent place. Competition is fierce, so fierce that some nationals publish their big-size papers on Saturdays to forestall the traditional Sunday bulkies.

The appeal of the top-selling tabloids relies on content and approach, the emphasis being on human interest and sensational stories (especially in the world of showbiz), sport and unpretentious light-hearted family entertainment. The tabloids report stories in more condensed or shortened versions than the heavier papers do, and offer many more illustrations. Tabloid Sundays adopt the same pattern as their daily counterparts.

Currently leading the field in circulation terms are the following national daily papers:

Sun
1 Virginia Street
Wapping
London E1 9BD
tel 0171-782 4000
fax 0171-483 3235

Daily Mirror
1 Canada Square
Canary Wharf
London E14 5AP
tel 0171-510 3000
fax 0171-510 3405

Daily Star
245 Blackfriars Road
London SE1 9UX
tel 0171-928 8000
fax 0171-633 0244

Daily Mail
2 Derry Street
London W8 5TT
tel 0171-938 6000
fax 0171-937 3251

Daily Express
245 Blackfriars Road
London SE1 9UX
tel 0171-928 8000
fax 0171-633 0244

Daily Telegraph
1 Canada Square
Canary Wharf
London E14 5DT
tel 0171-538 5000
fax 0171-538 6242

Guardian
119 Farringdon Road
London EC1R 3ER
tel 0171-278 2332
fax 0171-837 2114

The Times,
1 Virginia Street
Wapping
London E1 9XN
tel 0171-782 5000
fax 0171-782 5988

Independent
1 Canada Square
Canary Wharf
London E14 5DL
tel 0171-293 2000
fax 0171-293 2435

Financial Times
1 Southwark Bridge
London SE1 9HL
tel 0171-873 3000
fax 0171-873 3076

And on Sundays:

News of the World
1 Virginia Street
Wapping
London E1 9XR
tel 0171-782 4000
fax 0171-782 4463

Sunday Mirror
1 Canada Square
Canary Wharf
London E14 5AP
tel 0171-293 3000
fax 0171-293 3405

The People
1 Canada Square
Canary Wharf
London E14 5AP
tel 0171-293 3201
fax 0171-293 3810

Mail on Sunday
2 Derry Street
London W8 5TT
tel 0171-938 6000
fax 0171-937 3745

Sunday Express
245 Blackfriars Road
London SE1 9UX
tel 0171-928 8000
fax 0171-620 1656

Sunday Times
1 Pennington Street
London E1 9XW
tel 0171-782 5000
fax 0171-782 5658

Sunday Telegraph
1 Canada Square
Canary Wharf
London E14 5DT
tel 0171-538 5000
fax 0171-538 6242

Observer
119 Farringdon Road
London EC1R 3ER
tel 0171-278 2332
fax 0171-837 2114

Independent on Sunday
1 Canada Square
Canary Wharf
London E14 5DL
tel 0171-293 2000
fax 0171-293 2043

The European (published
weekly on Thursdays)
200 Gray's Inn Road
London WC1X 8NE
tel 0171-418 7777
fax 0171-713 1840

Among the top regional dailies are:

Evening Standard
2 Derry Street
London W8 5EE
tel 0171-938 6000
fax 0171-937 3273

Express & Star
51–53 Queen Street
Wolverhampton
West Midlands WV1 3BU
tel (01902) 313131
fax (01902) 319721

Evening Mail
28 Colmore Circus
Birmingham B4 6AX
tel 0121-236 3366
fax 0121-233 0271

Manchester Evening News
164 Deansgate
Manchester M60 2RD
tel 0161-832 7200
fax 0161-832 5351

Liverpool Echo
Old Hall Street
Liverpool L69 3EB
tel 0151-227 2000
fax 0151-236 4682

Belfast Telegraph
124–144 Royal Avenue
Belfast BT1 1EB
tel (01232) 264000
fax (01232) 554506

Daily Record
Anderston Quay
Glasgow
Strathclyde G3 8DA
tel 0141-248 7000
fax 0141-242 3340

Evening Times
195 Albion Street
Glasgow G1 1QP
tel 0141-552 6255
fax 0141-553 1355

Press & Journal
Lang Stracht
Mastrick
Aberdeen AB9 8AF
tel (01224) 690222
fax (01224) 663575

The Herald
195 Albion Street
Glasgow G1 1QP
tel 0141-552 6255
fax 0141-552 2288

Courier & Advertiser
80 Kingsway East
Dundee DD4 8SL
tel (01382) 223131
fax (01382) 454590

The ethnic press now serves an important number of readers and includes the following:

Asharq Al Awsat
(Arabic daily)
184 High Holborn
London WC1V 7AP
tel 0171-831 8181
fax 0171-831 2310

The Asian Age
(Asian daily)
Suite 4
55 Park Lane
London W1Y 3DB
tel 0171-304 4028
fax 0171-304 4029

Caribbean Times
(weekly for ex-Caribbeans)
141–149 Fonthill Road
London N4 3HF
tel 0171-281 1191
fax 0171-263 9656

Punjabi Darpan
(weekly Punjabi)
36 Trent Avenue
London W5 4TL
tel 0181-840 3534
fax 0181-579 3180

Siyu
(Chinese daily)
16 Nicholas Street
Manchester M1 4EJ
tel 0161-228 0420
fax 0161-228 3739

Hurriyet
(Turkish daily)
35 D'Arblay Street
London W1V 3FE
tel 0171-734 1211
fax 0171-255 1106

Daily Deshbarata
(Bengali daily)
170 Brick Lane
London E1 6RU
tel 0171-377 1584
fax 0171-247 9299

Who owns what

Britain's fastest-growing newspaper chain is Trinity International Holdings which (since the purchase of Thomson Regional Newspapers and a string of smaller companies) now commands 125 titles, boasting a combined circulation of some 9 million copies. Several of the papers listed above are owned by partnerships of proprietors or by individuals, but most are in the hands of limited liability companies. The best-known independent newspaper is the *Guardian*, owned by the Scott Trust, which was established in 1936 to maintain the high journalistic and commercial standards of C. P. Scott, editor and proprietor of the then *Manchester Guardian*. Now titled the Guardian Media Group, it also controls the *Observer* and more than 50 local papers. In 1986 the *Independent* was launched as another single-venture enterprise and is to this day funded by journalists anxious to avoid what they fear as manipulation by a proprietor.

Notwithstanding such individual enterprises, a handful of 'giants' now own and run the majority of Britain's national and provincial papers. As many of the giants' empires also include commercial involvement all over the world – in television, communications, shipping, property, airlines, oil, insurance and high-level commerce, for example – tremendous power in the world of communications rests in their hands. Your weekly paper may seem just the local rag you view with some affection but wouldn't credit with much importance beyond its immediate circulation area: in reality it is probably a small cog in a very big wheel.

The huge power of newspaper chains has been a major factor in British journalism, and anxiety about too much power being controlled by the same proprietor surfaces every time there is a newspaper merger, and so it should. It is illegal to transfer a newspaper or newspaper assets to a proprietor whose newspapers have an average daily circulation, with that of the newspaper to be taken over, of 500,000 or more copies, without the written consent of the Secretary of State for Industry, but the big moguls search to find loopholes in legal complexities. Sometimes they win, sometimes they lose.

Today Rupert Murdoch, a native Australian who is now a naturalised American (estimated to be America's 13th-richest citizen, incidentally, with a personal fortune in excess of £250 million) heads the giant media conglomerate News Corporation which owns the *Sun, News of the World, The Times* and *Sunday Times*. Besides controlling more than a third of British national newspaper circulation, he also owns more than 20 American newspapers, a dozen in Australia and has substantial magazine holdings in many countries including Britain.

Mirror Group Newspapers own the *Daily Mirror, Sunday Mirror, The People, Daily Record, Sunday Mail, The Sporting Life* and the English language *China Daily*, among many other smaller titles, and 40 per cent of Scottish Television. Former chairman the late Robert Maxwell founded and owned Pergamon Press (who published no fewer than 550 periodicals under various imprints), owned Britain's largest network of cable channels and had wide interests in broadcasting and television.

The Daily Mail and General Trust, a company run by descendants of Lord Northcliffe, controls the *Daily Mail, Mail on Sunday*, London *Evening Standard* and a string of regional titles. The trust also has holdings in West Country Television, Reuters News Agency, Teletext and local radio.

United News and Media is in charge of 13 per cent of all national paper circulation with the *Daily Express, Sunday Express, Daily Star, Yorkshire Post* and more than 80 local newspapers spread all over the country.

Through the Canadian company Hollinger, Conrad Black controls the *Daily Telegraph*, the *Sunday Telegraph* and *The Spectator*.

In a class of its own, as yet small but perhaps of greater significance in the future, is the unique concept of *The European*, a pan-European newspaper launched by Robert Maxwell in mid-May 1990 with printing in Hungary and West Germany as well as in this country. It is owned by the Barclay twins, who bought The Scotsman Publications from Thomson Regional Newspapers in 1995.

The provincial press

When it comes to circulation and readership figures, the latter on average three times higher than the former, according to the quarterly figures published by the Audit Bureau of Circulations (Black Prince Yard, 207–209 High Street, Berkhamsted, Herts HP4 1AD *tel* (01442) 870800 *fax* (01442) 877407), the regional and local press knock the nationals into a shredding machine. About 20 million people read a regional morning or evening newspaper, more than 25 million buy a local weekly paper, and most of them read both. At the latest count there were almost 2,000 provincial papers, including more than 80 morning and evening regional dailies, mostly published from city centres, 380 paid-for weeklies and an estimated 1,000 'freesheets', generally weeklies but some published less frequently. Gone are the days, moreover, when freesheets were considered below the salt and no self-respecting journalist would write for them; now, with few exceptions, they've pulled up their socks and worked hard to make themselves worthy of everyone's market study.

The huge provincial press thrives on regional and local events, while the nationals concentrate on national and international news flooding in from correspondents, news agencies and other sources. Should an important news story break in its circulation area, a local paper will of course give the story closer coverage than national papers can – and the supporting features relevant to the story will be of enormous interest to local readers. But how, you may ask, is the freelance writer to be prepared for, say, an unexploded bomb being found in an old cellar, a local man winning the national lottery or a burglar breaking into a house and holding a family hostage for two days? You may have the answer in your own reach. Your file of press cuttings about your district just might be able to tell you if other old bombs have been found in the town, where, when, and what happened to them; the enterprising writer could have a collection of rags-to-riches stories waiting for the right moment; information about other cases of families being held hostage in their homes will most certainly be dug out by somebody who writes the front page story in your local paper – so why shouldn't it be you? Noting the differences in the way national, regional and local papers cover the same event – perhaps a major disaster – is rewarding market study. If it's a story of more than local importance, it ought to be you who writes it up for the regional paper as well; you will have all the facts ready at your fingertips, you will know the area and be able to contact the people involved.

All the leading evening papers boast large circulation figures. More people buy the London *Evening Standard* every day than buy *The Times*; the Birmingham *Evening Mail* and Wolverhampton's *Express & Star* both sell in excess of 200,000 copies a day. Local Sunday regional papers are also big sellers, the top two being Dundee's *Sunday Post* and Glasgow's *Sunday Mail*.

Local papers

Local papers flourish all over the country: they are important in major cities, the grass roots of the provincial press – and even small communities that regard themselves as independent from either are proud of their own publications. Whatever else local papers may be, they are all intensely local in appeal. As you study them more closely you will realise 'local' does not mean 'narrow-minded' or 'parochial' in its pejorative sense. Broadly speaking they exist for three reasons: to strengthen community 'togetherness' with pride in past or current achievements, for instance; to protect it by highlighting shortcomings in local street lighting, say, or allowing readers to voice protests about children's playgrounds; and (perhaps most important of the three) to inform readers. It almost goes without saying they must also interest and entertain them as well. The best papers work hard for their success; the *Bolton Evening News* was the first regional evening paper to run for 24 hours a day, 7 days a week, and more soon followed this example.

As there are so many of them, local papers are the hardest to list and it's virtually impossible to detail what they want from freelance writers; yet of all newspaper markets they present the easiest target. You may be weary of the old advice to *study the market*, but writing for local papers proves how essential it is. Read your local paper regularly and you can hardly help but get the 'feel' of it; you know how its mind works and you know what the reaction of the people who are reading it will be to its various parts. If this is 'market study', call it absorption or instinct instead if you like. However it's described, this is knowing a market in the depth that shows you what and how to write for it.

Think of your local paper not with an indulgent smile but as if it is somone talking to a friend, or a few thousand friends, as indeed it is. We have no difficulty making casual conversation with our acquaintances about titbits of what's happening in the area, scraps of gossip and chatter of mutual interest, and we should feel equally at ease with the 'local rag'. Just remember how distanced from it you felt when you first moved to where you live now or the scant interest you can summon when you read someone else's paper in an area you don't know. A local paper is exactly what it wants to be – something you can relax with, a good friend until you consign it to its afterlife of wrapping up the fish and chips or lining the wheelie-bin.

Find your own markets

Over and over again I have proved that nothing is more successful than finding markets for yourself; catch them in their infancy (experience and experimentation will sometimes tell you how viable they may be in the long term) and you've a good chance not only of 'getting in on the ground floor' but also of persuading the editor to mould the paper just a little in the way you would like it to go. Seeing your own column or page in every issue, and knowing it's only there because you made it, is a great boost to the confidence. Always watch out for news of papers about to be launched – and think of ways in which you can contribute to them. Does your head instantly fill with ideas for regular features, articles, original columns, or – at the very least – query letters to the editor? And does excitement mount as you get started on them?

Wild as the idea may seem when you read this – why not launch your own market? A colleague of mine is presently engaged in doing just this. Not with paper, print costs, hiring staff or premises and all the other major capital expenditure involved in starting even the most modest publication. He read a plea on the Internet (see page 109) from a merchant seaman that went like this: 'Is it possible to receive any daily newspapers via e-mail? We work on a ship for a month at a time, effectively cut off from the world. We do a daily blink (see page

157) to collect our Internet mail. An English daily paper coming in with this feed would be most welcome.' My friend set to work.

Anyone online can read the *Electronic Telegraph* or the *Guardian Online* section as web pages, and other leading papers are available on this medium. Where there's a market, there's a way . . .

Freesheets

In the United Kingdom we can expect (and often cannot avoid) something like 50 million free papers pushed through our letterboxes at regular intervals. More than half of them are free 'extras' from the same stables as our paid-for weeklies, which is perhaps why the business of issuing both is known to the trade as 'total publishing'. These freesheets, as we call them, vary greatly in size, quality and frequency of publication (although most are weeklies) and, as in the national paper industry, ownership tends to be concentrated in the hands of a few large companies. Free papers are read by 80 per cent of all adults, and there are probably as many openings for freelance writers in the freesheet pages as they have the ingenuity to produce. Where the paid-for weeklies will have established correspondents in most circulation areas (again, not all, so there are often openings there), freesheets largely depend on the man/woman in the street for a supply of news, coverage of forthcoming events, topical and non-topical features – and whatever else the enterprising writer may create. Therein lies a freelance's opportunity; a glance at any freesheet page will readily reveal openings to the market-seeking eye of a determined contributor; closer careful study and some resourceful work will be the first step to supplying what is wanted.

If there are two or more freesheets covering your area, study them individually and together. Noting their similarities and their differences will be invaluable. Incidentally, just as the idea has died that writing for freesheets is beneath the 'real' journalist's dignity, so has that more distasteful idea that 'frees don't pay'; nowadays most of them do. Freesheets are big business and of course their contributors should and do expect to be treated as 'proper' writers.

More . . .

Everybody knows newspapers are printed in ink that quickly makes your fingers dirty on the type of paper referred to as 'newsprint' and that magazines use thicker, glossier paper and have their pages stapled, sewn or stuck together. So what does that make the weekend colour supplements which have no existence separate from their big national parents? And what about all the papers/magazines devoted to readers of specialist trades or religious groups, material published by companies for their employees or hobbyist papers for their enthusiasts? Many of these are printed on newsprint, but are they newspapers? Some time ago I sold a regular column to the *Morning Advertiser*, which is the organ of the Licensed Victuallers' trade and the smallest national daily, but is still commonly referred to as a 'magazine'. Since parts of this book are applicable to magazines as well as to newspapers, it would seem churlish to leave these grey areas on the copy-taster's spike. While some of the greys pay nothing, and contributors would not expect otherwise, there is no doubt that there are circumstances in which going grey can be quite profitable.

Syndication

Get into the habit of looking for markets and they pop up everywhere. Several large overseas cities run English-language newspapers, and syndication here and overseas can continue to earn smaller sums for writers ready to hand over copy already paid-for to syndication agencies.

Syndication is another way of finding new markets – but for already published material of your own. This is not only possible but ethically acceptable, and its secret is that many newspapers have clearly defined and limited circulation areas. So editor Alan Bloggs in Ayrshire won't be at all worried if you have sold the article he's buying to editor Frank Knight in Penzance, because nobody in the Ayrshire circulation area is likely to see newspapers published in Penzance. For the same reason Frank Knight of Penzance won't be annoyed at publication in distant Ayrshire, even if he ever gets to hear about it. If an Ayrshire reader, by chance visiting relations in Penzance, reads what he already read in last week's paper at home, he will only feel a slight superiority that his home paper 'got there first', and no harm is done to either title.

All the same, if copy is being syndicated, i.e. has already been sold at least once elsewhere, you should indicate this when offering it to any other editor. The fact that it has already met with approval somewhere else is likely to commend it to him: it's of proven marketable quality. He also knows it won't cost him as much as would non-syndicated copy, since you expect to be paid for it several times.

In this type of marketing a query letter is essential. Use it to introduce yourself (briefly) and your wares (more fully) to newspaper editors in widely differing parts of the country. Freesheets buy a huge amount of syndicated material. It's a good idea to consult a marketing guide (see below) to study where newspaper groups may mean circulation areas overlap; purchase by a group may involve passing your copy to several titles within the group. Who would guess, for example, that papers in Portsmouth and Sunderland are under the same umbrella?

Because the fee for individual sales will be modest, it is not cost-effective to try syndicating work that doesn't have a better-than-average chance of being accepted. Maybe it's the comparatively humble reward that has given syndication a poor image. But weigh up the advantages: each payment is only part of what the copy may earn in its lifetime, there is no extra research or writing to be done and your expense with each submission is small. Photocopying the copy and a short covering letter to recipients have been the only work; envelopes and postage the total cost. You could call syndication money for jam. It is particularly easy if you have a large stock of useful copy (dispatch a dozen or more items together for maximum impact and minimum trouble) and don't mind the jam being rather thinly spread on each piece.

There is also the other side of the coin to consider and that is the value you place on your time. To my mind syndication is only worthwhile if it can be accomplished as well as other useful work, not instead of it. You might prefer to let someone else do the work of syndication for you. There are many agencies and some only take freelance copy. Their usual terms are a 50/50 split on all sales. The leading agencies are highly commercialised enterprises. Some state they're looking for professional writers with 'international minds', and most operate on a basic 20–25 per cent handling charge. This means they send lists of ideas provided by their contributors to editors. The paper might then take up several ideas and want further details. All this will take place before any article is completed and the agency (taking its share of any fee going) might first pass your copy on to another agency. At this level it's big business and so are the slices taken from the rewards. At the click of a keyboard what started as a £250 fee can shrink by 50 per cent of 50 per cent less deductions for this and that – and reach you as just £20. Only you can decide whether it is worth it or not.

As for overseas newspapers – there are not many published in English. Exceptions are those specifically for English-speaking expatriates and for people working overseas, the latter usually only being catered for in this respect when they are concentrated in a relatively small area and there are plenty of them: publishing economics seldom allow papers to be viable otherwise.

Market guides

There are several reliable sources of market news. The main ones are:

- *Writers' & Artists' Yearbook* (A & C Black Ltd, 35 Bedford Row, London WC1R 4JH *tel* 0171-242 0946 *fax* 0171-831 8478)
  Recommended by the Society of Authors, this long-established vade mecum is in two main sections: markets, and general information for writers.

- *Willings Press Guide* (Reed Information Services)
  Available in most reference libraries.

- *Freelance Market News* (Sevendale House, 7 Dale Street, Manchester M1 1JB *tel* 0161-228 2362 *fax* 0161-228 3533)
  Mainly covering magazines but some newspapers are included.

- *The Media Guide* (Fourth Estate Limited, 6 Salem Road, London W2 4BU *tel* 0171-727 8993 *fax* 0171-792 3176)
  A superb guide and source book, written from inside the profession by working journalists.

- *Benn's Media* (Miller Freeman Information Services, Riverbank House, Angel Lane, Tonbridge, Kent TN9 1SE *tel* (01732) 364422 *fax* (01732) 367301)
  Here are all the newspapers in the UK, both national and

regional, with circulation details, key management, editorial and advertisement executives. Cover prices and advertising rates are also listed.

- *British Rate and Data* (33–39 Bowling Green Lane, London EC1R 0DA *tel* 0171-505 8274 *fax* 0171-505 8201)
  Media facts are at your fingertips in this (expensive) monthly publication which is primarily a marketing handbook. Its comprehensive coverage includes all national and regional dailies, Sunday and weekly papers and freesheets.

Sources such as these are well known and open to all writers, so competition for the markets mentioned in their pages may be stiff. Make sure, of course, that all the references you consult are as up to date as possible.

You are not likely to miss the arrival (or closure) of a national paper, such is the publicity given to these events, but you have to keep watch over newspaper births and deaths (and sometimes, marriages) in local and provincial journalism. Any local library should be able to tell you what is published to cover your area or the area you are interested in, but a more practical way of finding the very latest in local publishing is to ask your newsagent. Make him a friend and waylay him for a chat at a time he's not busy. He'll probably be delighted to find someone sufficiently interested in newspapers to ask him about them. A close notebook-in-hand study of his shelves, if nothing better, will give you local information.

While published lists of titles and addresses inevitably date quickly, *British Rate and Data,* known in the business as 'BRAD', probably remains the UK's most reliable guide to circulation figures and readership profiles.

Even when you think you've identified and located regional and local papers you can't relax. A few months ago, in the departure lounge of a major British airport, I picked up a newspaper abandoned by another traveller. It was one I had never seen before, nor even heard about. I have now sold half-a-dozen small items to the editor, who asks to see more copy from me on several topics. What is the paper? You may find it mentioned in the pages of this book . . .

3. What to Write

A list of topics to write about would a) fill the rest of the book, and b) scarcely be topical as I have no way of knowing what's going to be in the news and public awareness when you read this. Although you may be prepared to devote much effort and research to a project and bring originality to it, mere lists of ideas can encourage stultified and channelled thinking from the start; countless writers before you have stared at similar lists and tried to grasp the last whiff of inspiration from them; countless editors have seen (and rejected) the results. More is needed than an idea. Finding one in the first place is most likely to be successful when it arrives in your head jockeying for priority, albeit loosely, with a notion of how you're going to develop it and turn it into – what? For therein lies the other major decision to be made: *what* are you going to write?

Give yourself time to think about it. Write an idea down but then let it grow in your head before writing it up – the latter has the seal of finality on it and it may be a mistake to give your idea too much substance too early, especially if you don't have a particular (or any) deadline. When you can distance yourself sufficiently from what you intend to write, the idea may strike you as old hat after all; but put your creative originality to work and it should take on a new lease of life. Just as your personality makes you different from anyone else, so the viewpoint, attitude, treatment, tone, mood, voice, the *character* you give an idea will make it yours alone.

People who know nothing about writing imagine we only write what we want to write. We can pick and choose, they assume, and we don't write anything we don't want to write. Nobody's making us do it, after all. That would be an adequate philosophy for a writer with an annual output of a couple of Letters to the Editor, say, or a once-yearly report in a local charity booklet; 'tea-time' writers can indulge in the luxury of choosing how much to write and what to write about – and

41

good luck to every one. If you're in this writing business as a serious endeavour you'll have a different approach. A fisherman baits his hook not with what he likes, but with what fish like. There are many hard lessons to learn about freelancing, and one of the toughest is that you have to write not just the stories that appeal to you, but the stories that will sell. When you enjoy working on those as well (and if you're a journalist at heart, you will) that can only be counted as a bonus.

Whatever laws are quoted as paths to success (some of which gain greater fame for their advocates than does their literary output), one is supreme and irrefutable: the only certain entrée to the columns of a newspaper is a good story well written. If you constantly remind yourself that it's what readers want that sells, you will instinctively know what to give them – because (if for no other reason) it's probably what you want for yourself. To enjoy good health and happy personal relationships, to earn and save enough money, to have a roof over your head and most of the material goods you want (within reason), to have other people respect and admire you, to get a good job and do well in it, to safeguard your children – are these not the normal aims and desires of the great general public? Most of us, wishing no harm or hardship to others, care most about self-interest. Write about that natural wish among readers, especially telling them how to satisfy it, and you'll always give them what they want to read. And when readers want it, editors buy it.

Out of thin air

Ideas are everywhere, but there is no real substitute for studying the papers you'd like to write for. Analyse their content, their page layout and format and try to find out why they print the features/news items/fillers (or whatever you are interested in) that they do. Even this market study isn't infallible, for at best it can only reveal what they printed and were interested in *yesterday*. As for what they'll want tomorrow and the next day and the next . . . No matter where you live or work, whom you meet, how you spend your time or what your hobbies and interests may be, there's a story. Feature, filler, news item, article, review, regular series, specialist column, interview, diary item, letter, anecdote, profile, preview – there is always something to be written. Never make the beginner's mistake of writing and asking for a sheet of guidelines (which many magazines are happy to supply) unless you want to be considered too lazy to do your own market study and too slow and amateurish for a weekly paper, let alone a daily.

It is rather daunting to realise that there is no such thing as a new idea. I was born knowing nothing at all. So any knowledge I have acquired since that day has been absorbed from what I have read, heard, understood, deduced and (if you wish to think of it this way) 'copied' from what originated with someone else. How about you? Realising that nobody else in the world sees through your eyes or with your precise perception of what you are seeing or hearing makes all the difference.

Whatever you write, never forget the purpose of doing so. Thought must be structured before writing can be, and giving your brain an intensive storming session can often work wonders. Try this:

1 Sit in your most comfortable chair with just a paper and pencil on your lap and let yourself drift into a half day-dream. Don't consciously force your mind to think up ideas but when it does, jot them down as quickly as you can, in any order and heedless of any lack of sense or logic.

2 When you 'come to', start considering what you've written in a more practical light. Are the ideas viable, fresh and interesting? Can any be developed to fit your intended market? At reasonable cost and in time?

3 If you get stuck or the day-dreaming session seems a waste of time, try again. With practice many people find some of their best ideas this way – although others gain nothing productive for their efforts. Some even fall asleep. If problems arise with any idea you decide to work on, try to think of a better approach, perhaps turning it round and taking an entirely different slant.

4 Don't judge during the day-dreaming stage. It may surprise you with some big ideas; giving yourself occasional time to dream is important.

Seizing opportunities

Never let an idea, let alone a completed project, persuade you it is working out well when your heart, your head or your increasing journalistic instinct tells you it isn't. I hate the phrase

'It'll do' in this context: it is usually an excuse, when what is needed is the extra effort to get the story right. Don't be content too easily.

Would you decline a chance to work on a story because you don't know anything about the subject? I hope not. It may turn out to be more fun than work: you never know. An editor asked me to fill in for another writer who had been taken ill and write about a band of duck-devotees holding up the traffic to let squads of ducks cross the road in safety from one part of a country park to another. Many times I'd seen ducks gathering at a particular spot by the side of the road and had prayed they would stay there. But I had no idea they were trained to wait until their personal crossing wardens arrived to see them to the other side. Adopting one of the tenets of a journalist's craft and never being afraid to ask anyone for information, I discovered the local police could not grant official permission to the kindly patrols when they wanted to hold up the traffic but had promised they would only take action against them if motorists complained about being asked to stop. The duck-devotees had done their teaching job well; so impeccably behaved were their quacking charges in waddling across that motorists were only amused and intrigued. My story (and some pix) in the local paper (and further afield) ensured everyone in the area knew about the web-footed crossing patrols. Extra volunteers joined the others in duckherding the ducks (is that an appropriate word?) and someone suggested there should be a crossing sign showing a little green duck when it was safe to cross. It was all harmless fun which everyone enjoyed as much as I did.

On less frivolous topics you may need to do a proportion of your work before ever writing a word. A thinly researched article quickly lands on the reject pile if another author has taken more time and trouble to delve into the subject. That's what reference libraries are for, and there are enormous facilities for researching anything and everything. What's more, as your pile of researched material grows, so will your interest and enthusiasm. To write well you have to be interested in what you're writing, or at least make yourself interested. If you're not, why should anyone else be?

An escape from a topic you're bored with? An esoteric subject that suddenly intrigues you? A story whose main attraction is that it's what you've always wanted to write? Beware. These could be reasons for your story not selling because they're the wrong reasons for writing it. Are you therefore condemning yourself to nothing but monotony and feigned interest? By no means. There are some fortuitous results of getting stuck into this freelancing business; success is more consistent when you persevere, and the more you do the more you find you're enjoying it. Many years ago a journalist with worldwide experience and credits to match advised me thus: 'Streams of workable ideas come only to those constantly engaged in creative work.' Those workable ideas are what we want to write, but firstly they must be what readers want to read.

Chance and pegs

The best ideas often occur by chance. I happened to come across a man who mentioned, in the course of a conversation about publicity, that he had been an advertising copywriter in the 1970s and had worked on an advertising jingle of the day for the Burnley Building Society. Then he gave a little laugh. 'You know who worked on it with me? Salman Rushdie.' Suddenly I had an idea (the unusual earlier jobs of well-known authors) and all I had to do was to make it workable with research and planning. I also had a 'peg' because Salman Rushdie was very much in the news at the time.

The previous sentence is very important in the world of newspapers. Very little copy, be it feature, filler or in any other format, is wanted unless it is tied to an event or a person in the news at the time of publication. Everything set before an editor's eyes needs to be hung on a peg, i.e. relevant to an item of news already in the public eye.

The copy itself need not be brand new; it may be lurking in your store cupboard or even unwritten in your head waiting for the right peg to present itself. On one such occasion the escape (and recapture) of a tiger cub from a Home Counties zoo was in the news. Keepers explained the cub had probably escaped because he was bored and wanted a bit of excitement. Out came my true (and *recent*) story about keepers at Edinburgh Zoo who had designed a special exercise machine to occupy lazy cheetahs who weren't getting enough exercise. The machine hauled a dead rabbit along by a system of motorised pulleys, encouraging the cheetahs to rush round their enclosures in pursuit. But cheetahs aren't silly. After a while they learned the rabbit would appear at regular intervals whatever they did, so they ceased bothering to chase it. Only when it appeared irregularly did they show interest again. But that meant the keepers had to crank the machine by hand, which was hot and tiring work. I was able to end my story with the good news that all the keepers at Edinburgh Zoo were in excellent physical condition and happy to help the Home Counties in any way they could.

A newspaper may be only ink on paper but it's alive; luckier than the mayfly with its three hours, and sometimes given a whole fortnight or even longer. It feeds on the topicality and originality its makers can give it, and on the quality of the writing on its pages. Aim to please the readers and the editor will also be pleased because he wants the same thing, although many I've come across admit they don't know what they want until they see it. It is to our advantage that newspapers do so much more than report news. They also provide commentaries on the news, promote or decry various public policies, offer special information and advice to readers, and most include features such as comic strips, cartoons and serialised books. Serialising a book by a famous name, incidentally, can cost a leading paper as much as £100,000. Newspapers are aimed at a mass readership. In addition to the serious news of the day, they contain something to appeal to most men, women and children – and all this means there is plenty of opportunity for freelances, both in what to write and what ideas to write about.

A writer friend of mine laughingly recounts telling another of her success in a local publication. 'That's a good market,' was the second writer's reply. 'They'll take anything.' Not quite the compliment the speaker intended it to be, perhaps, but don't think that higher standards make freelancing more difficult, for the very reverse is true; the higher the standards the fewer are the writers able to write well enough for publication, so the competition is less, not more. Let the challenge of higher standards bring out the best in your working ability.

Features

Sometimes the word 'article' is hardly used on the editorial floor in a newspaper office. Copy that might be referred to as an 'article' is more likely to be called a 'feature'. But a feature is not an article made to sound grand, for the terms are virtually synonymous. I make the point here only to clarify what a features editor or someone on his staff is almost certainly talking about when he refers to a 'feature', an 'article' or even a 'feature article'. In this book I use the first two terms and confess the tautologous third bewilders me.

Staff on newspapers tend to assume that a feature is copy written by a journalist whose work is well known to readers through appearing in the paper regularly or frequently. It is likely to include his informed point of view on the topic because, goes the logic, readers feel at home with the writer and understand him. Being regarded as almost a friend, the feature writer deftly balances his innate emotional response to whatever he is writing with his practical training of how to write it most effectively. Not that all readers approve of his words, of course, but if they provoke lively discussion in Letters to the Editor, so much the better. The feature writer is someone whose work readers want to read, warts and all, a part of the paper they like and perhaps one of the main reasons why they keep buying it.

A series of single articles or even one standing alone may also be spoken of as a 'feature' since anyone writing it will by implication be something of an expert on the topic. Naturally a one-off article has just as valid a place in a paper as anything else the editor wants to print – or it wouldn't be there. So I regret the assumption I've occasionally encountered from inexperienced freelances that an 'article' is a minor piece expected merely to skim over the subject with two or three well-known or ill-researched facts, the writer's personal opinion and a lot of light-weight chit-chat. Nothing will get published with that half-hearted benchmark – and it doesn't deserve to. Call it what you wish, anything you send to the features editor of a newspaper needs to stop him in his tracks ('We must buy this!') or at least lure him enough to contact you about development of a point here, getting a pic for a par there, and so on.

A further characteristic of a feature is that it is usually tagged to a news event. It may, for instance, give background information on a running story about prison rioting when there's been trouble at a nearby prison, reveal past histories of an unusual medical condition recently occurring in the district, or dig out some awkward facts following the disappearance of funds from a local charity's coffers. Whatever its theme, be careful your story is not out of date, having been overtaken by more recent news.

You may already have interested the editor or features editor with an exploratory letter, but if you go in 'cold' it is even more important to hit him right between the eyes. You've made yourself an expert, remember, even if only a temporary one. Features may be based entirely on facts, but it is their relevance to *people* that makes them viable. Write a piece about the first impressions of Eastern Europeans on seeing the shops in the West, with plenty of human interest and quotes, of course; or the increase in business for UK seaside hotel landladies due to airport flight delays. Make yourself the bringer of comfort, an inspiration, an instructor, or a wallower in nostalgia. Give readers the latest facts about education, medical services, local transport, job opportunities – all are important to people, aren't they? There truly is no end to what you might write about. Of course the old advice given to beginners is still pertinent: write about what you know. But that doesn't mean fill your piece with little more than your own opinion and personal experiences. It is boring to be in the company of someone who talks about nothing but himself. Readers are interested in how what they're reading will relate to themselves.

It pays to look ahead, particularly in ways other writers may not. The traditional events on which countless hopefuls 'tag' their articles may be easy to write about but are often difficult to sell simply because they have been sucked dry and written to death. Original freelance copy on an editor's desk is more welcome than a tea-break. Once you get your mind in gear, finding what to write about at the right time will never be a problem.

A good feature writer can write about virtually anything. When you do so, make it strong: make them laugh, cry, want to know more, swear, feel encouraged, understand something or someone better, agree, disagree – or whatever you choose – but make sure they do or feel *something*. That's what feature writing is all about.

News

Have you heard the tale of Jack and Pete who were playing golf together on a small green when they saw an amateur player score a hole-in-one three times in a few minutes? After congratulations had flowed in the clubhouse, Jack went home and told his wife about this remarkable feat over lunch. Pete didn't bother with the party in the clubhouse but hastily scribbled a few notes on the back of an envelope he found in his pocket and went straight to the nearest telephone. Local, regional and national papers paid handsomely for his story and would have paid a good deal more if he had also had a camera in his pocket at the time. The story was taken up by radio and television and earned headlines on all the sporting pages. Jack hasn't got and probably doesn't want a 'news-nose'; Pete's is developing well and will surely lead him on to bigger and better stories he'll be more prepared to exploit to the full when they occur. Most importantly, he's learned the value of timing when it comes to filing a news story. News makes up only 10 per cent of the space available in tabloids but a good deal more in the quality papers, so if you were Pete which of the nationals would you sell the story to after you'd let the local and regional papers have it?

Developing a news-nose isn't difficult if you are already keenly interested in people, what they do and what happens to them. In fact, once you get into the habit of spotting news you'll discover there's so much of it as to be an *embarras de richesses*. Then comes the art of selection, which also improves with experience of the markets waiting for news, and an understanding of the value of each potential news item.

Seizing opportunities is one thing, but you have to spot them first. Practise training your eyes to notice what's going on around you, especially small and at first sight unimportant things (although not missing the larger ones either) and then – instinctively, with time – bring everything down to news-nose level for quick appraisal and selection. A successful news reporter not only sees things other people miss, he also knows what to do with an unexpected news story. If you are at the scene of an accident or an emergency, this well-honed observation sense can prove invaluable, not only to you doing a job of work, but also to police, firemen, ambulancemen and anyone able to help unfortunate victims. Of course you will take notes as copiously and quickly as you can in the circumstances; then comes the writing of the story and getting it to the paper.

When speed is essential you will initially be guided by the deadline of your paper. If you are writing a news story for a regional evening paper, say, and it is ten o'clock in the morning, the phone is the only practical way of filing copy. If you haven't a mobile phone, find a telephone (a box for relative quietness and privacy, if possible), assemble your notes if there hasn't been time to write the whole story, and ring the paper. Ask for the News Desk. Small local papers may not have anywhere in the office manned solely for news, so tell whoever answers the phone that you have a news story for a copytaker. Anyone who can take copy over the phone should be able to get your story down. Submitting a news story to a paper with no imminent deadline is a less fraught affair, but news about something that by the time of publishing will be several days old is also less useful to a freelance. In the intervening time all papers will have set their own staff to cover any newsworthy stories. It may be hectic, but from the freelance's point of view the best news is that which happens at the right time – when it is inconvenient or too late for staff reporters to cover it.

Some can be bizarre. A village near my home has a long-standing grudge that there is no gas service to the villagers, although a gas main pipe runs beside the village street. Early one evening as I drove along it on my way to a theatre-reviewing job in the small town some five miles further ahead, there was a tremendous explosion. The dust cleared to reveal a huge hole gaping by the village street where two old cottages had been. They had disappeared as if some giant hand had bent down and scooped them up. Police and ambulancemen quickly established there had – amazingly – been nobody in either cottage and there was no loss of life in the village; traffic was diverted round country lanes and policemen ran to every other dwelling, warning that all fires must be extinguished immediately. A strong smell of gas hung in the air; the village that wanted gas had certainly got it. Satisfied not even a dog or cat had been hurt, I realised the story was mine; not anything to rock the European Parliament or raise questions in the House of Commons but, albeit less than earth-shattering (though in the literal sense that's exactly what it was), an exclusive front page news story. The theatre? Fortunately it was the first of a four-night run and a couple of quick phone calls deferred the job to the next evening.

Once you get into the habit of looking for news, you'll find it seems to be looking for you. There is plenty around and on occasions it actually demands your attention. Be sure it deserves it and don't let your imagination take over when realism is demanded. A young colleague found himself in a lot of trouble when, without anything of real interest to report, he foolishly invented little stories for 'NIBS' items (see page 158). Suddenly a couple were taken up by the nationals who wanted chapter and verse – and caught him out when he couldn't provide them.

Bad news is good news for newspapers. The *Washington Post* reported that the tragic explosion of the TWA800 flight soon after take-off from New York in 1996 made more Internet callers hungry for news than those who went online to follow the Olympic Games which were taking place at the same time. But it would be a pity to think you want nothing to do with news reporting if it is only concerned with death and disaster. However trite much of it might seem, the honest reporting of news does a great deal of good: it brings praise where it is due and rewards where they are deserved; gives valuable publicity to worthwhile causes; highlights injustice; warns innocent people of dangers; and, most important at all levels, tells readers the truth.

News writing can be dramatic, but frequently it is about something that is anticipated: a report of a council meeting, for instance, where an important decision is awaited affecting a keenly felt local issue. The meeting may come in the realm of general run-of-the-mill reporting and you may be there as an informal observer having made no prior contact with any paper to report anything. (You may also have taken the trouble to establish that there will be nobody else covering for the press either, so your field is clear if anything newsworthy occurs.) Then, perhaps, a shouting match develops between opposing camps, some council stalwarts walk out in disgust, someone accuses councillors of rigging the ballot on the issue in question, or the decision itself is hard to believe. Those are the times when you'll not just be writing a report but filing a news story, and if there is a paper coming out the next morning you, as a freelance, could find yourself the only person able to write it. It was a news story that would have gone unheeded and unreported without your quick-wittedness.

Specialist columns

Few assignments are bigger eaters of original ideas than regular daily or weekly spots in a newspaper. Papers fail or succeed by the quality of their columns, the best-read bits of the papers, so good columnists are assiduously courted and highly paid. Many freelances vow there is nothing more satisfying than a regular page/half page/column/corner all to themselves. This type of work has been one of my specialities for more years than I can recall, and I can vouch for the advantages of it. It is an arrangement that usually results from an approach made to an editor by the writer able to show convincing evidence of his ability to hold down a regular place in the paper. It's not a commission won without effort, often over a number of years; the editor will want to know you will be able to sustain an unlimited time at the job, that your copy will constantly be fresh and innovative, and, most importantly, that it will always arrive on time. But when happy about these criteria, many editors are only too glad to hand over responsibility for a portion of the paper and know they needn't worry about it any more.

Letting the editor know your worth by several times selling him other copy is a good basis for asking for a regular column (we'll refer to it as a 'column' even though it may be more or less) as it gives you a chance of impressing him with your efficiency and dedication. On other occasions editors may invite you, out of the blue; but however it begins, a regular column is not something to be accepted lightly. It is hard to build up a good reputation and even harder to live up to it every week, let alone every day.

Thinking you have a well of ideas that will never run dry is easy; tapping it day after day (or however frequently your column demands you do so) and finding it still full, or full enough, may be different. Fortunately, I've found wells do have the magic property of being able to refill themselves; somehow, tapping the well of ideas gets the brain filling it up at increasing speed. I must not complain, therefore, because my own regular columns have gradually but inexorably imposed on me an instinctive habit of filling their particular wells even when I no longer want to tap them or at least want a break from doing so. Whether visiting friends, going on holiday, or being ill in hospital, I can't stop the wells filling. As a theatre reviewer, even when I go to a show 'off duty' my mind is soon turning round the intro, shape and viewpoint of review copy. I hope you can switch your brain off more satisfactorily than I can, but if you are a slave to your head at least you will never run out of ideas.

Of equal importance is that your copy must never be late. Never? If you are whisked off for unexpected surgery or bereaved of a close family member nobody would expect you to keep up an uninterrupted supply. But relations coming to stay, taking your summer holiday, simply being too busy doing some-thing else – try these as excuses for late copy and your editor won't keep you for long. The same rule applies for all copy, not just regular columns: short of real and rare emergencies, *a dead-line must be kept.*

The secret of being able to accept deadlines and still sleep at night may be this: plan ahead carefully, know your own writing capacity in terms of the research you may have to do for a particular item and the time it is likely to take you to write it, and – the best safety net in my opinion – have plenty of copy ready at home in your private store. Keep some ready to file, more half ready and only waiting for up-to-date material, and yet more awaiting your attention any time to maintain the quality and quantity of work in the store cupboard.

So what types of regular columns are out there waiting? Their themes are boundless: nature, profiles of famous people, chess, horoscopes, crosswords, competitions, children's and women's pages, young mothers, pop music, pets, food – any-thing that interests people will make a good column. Travel, sport, motoring, business and finance are among the topics nearly always covered by staff writers (it's not hard to under-stand why) and contributions to these sections have to be exceptional, if not unique. Nevertheless, faint heart never won fair lady, despite well-established opposition, so don't fear to try your hand.

If the paper you choose doesn't already run a column on your topic you'll be in a better position than if you just contribute to one already run by somebody else. Regular columns can (and often do) involve you in other fascinating writing jobs. Mine have taken me on tasks overseas, on nationwide promotional tours, made me editor of annuals, given me more regular columns in other papers here and overseas as well as a lot of other work, and led to more pleasant surprises than I can recall. A column will get you known and your work constantly read and appreciated. There are pleasant by-products too. Everybody has a pet/recipe/life story or whatever is relevant (and much that isn't) and you should be ready for the feedback from readers. This can be one of the most rewarding aspects of column-running if you don't let it take up too much of your writing time. And what else? At the end of every month you are guaranteed a pre-negotiated regular fee without having to invoice anyone.

Reviewing

The very special task of reviewing books, drama, films, videos, radio and television programmes is not work for a newcomer to writing. Book reviewing, for example, is by no means as easy as it might seem. 'Sitting on the fence' won't do. Reviews should be decisive, for their purpose is to tell the readers whether they should buy the book or not – if not directly. Reviews must be interesting and lively without being patronising, and reviewers are usually allowed a week or ten days to read books and write their reviews. Someone famous in another sphere (a politician or a top sportsman, say) might be invited to review one book a week, to attract readers with the name of the reviewer rather than his ability to review books, but the quality papers have their own trained and experienced staff reviewers. How, then, do you gain experience? For all categories of reviewing it is only at the discretion of the editor (or features editor, for reviews usually come under his aegis) that you may be given a chance. If you've read this far you will know the only way to build up a solid reputation is to keep writing the copy he wants when (or preferably just before) he wants it; in other words by demonstrating your professionalism.

An editor is also wary of offering a reviewing job to an unknown for fear of upsetting his staff who may be well qualified to do it. Think too of the author, the playwright, the radio writer or the television scriptwriter who finds his work inadequately covered. A bad review by a professional reviewer is fair enough; a poorly written one by someone who doesn't know what he's doing is not. One of my worst recollections of theatre reviewing is finding myself sitting next to a young man covering for another paper who innocently confided to me that he had never before seen a stage show or even set foot in a theatre. Common politeness battled with horror as I almost sank through the seat. Pity the playwright, the producer, the cast and everyone else. Most of all, perhaps, pity the young man.

Fillers

A filler is a small item, often just one or two sentences, used to fill up a little space in the paper. Writers may complain that the new technology, with its more efficient page layout, leaves fewer small spaces for fillers, but as in all marketing it is a matter of finding your own openings. Distinguish between news and general fillers, as a newspaper may confine itself to one variety.

Facts and figures make good copy for small regular corners. These bits and pieces of writing help to keep the mind ticking over in the right direction even if in themselves they are small fare. Faced with a daily journey to and from a newspaper office, I promised myself it would provide at least two fillers a day, which it did quite easily. You could try the same; write them out later and file them to a paper when you've amassed a good collection. A colleague satisfies competition addicts with a special corner currently running in the *Daily Mail*. She features one consumer competition every day, giving details of what it is, how to win the prizes it offers, and its closing date.

To a freelance writer nothing observed or overheard is ever wasted. For example, the British Library moved more than 12 million books and manuscripts from the old Bloomsbury site to the new one at St Pancras. The longest word in the *Oxford English Dictionary* is floccipaucinihilipilification but what does it mean? Such snippets can be fascinating – particularly when hung on a peg that makes them so: on their own they could make readers put the paper down with a sigh and say, 'So what?'

Make 'em laugh

As a filler of the non-news type may be a mini-anecdote, so an anecdote on its own may be something to lighten a reader's heart, especially when it is combined with humour. Make 'em laugh and you'll have editors eating out of your hand. However serious your chosen topic, readers will view it with greater affection if it – momentarily only, perhaps – makes them smile.

Another friend makes readers of a religious paper laugh with gems from her 'howlers' collection (which is always being topped up), captured from local pamphlets and notice-boards, such as:

- Don't let worry kill you, the church will help.
- On Easter Sunday Miss Jones will come forward and lay an egg on the altar.
- Mrs Smith will now sing 'Put me in my little bed', accompanied by the vicar.
- The church ladies have cast-off clothing of every kind and can be seen in the church hall on Wednesday.

This experienced columnist also relates funny stories of goings-on behind the scenes in a country rectory, but she laughs at herself with the recollection of how, even in such an apparently light-hearted spot in the paper, she once found herself taken to task for inaccuracy. It concerned her tale of two vicars from neighbouring parishes who regularly met to discuss their work and problems.

The younger one was sadly telling the other that his bicycle had been stolen and he felt it likely that one of his congregation was the thief. His friend had a solution. 'In your sermon next Sunday,' he suggested, 'take the Ten Commandments as your theme. When you reach "thou shalt not steal" just look up and the guilt on the thief's face will identify him.'

At their next meeting the older vicar asked if his plan had worked.

'I have my bicycle back,' the younger man said, and shuffled uneasily. 'I dwelt on the Ten Commandments but at "thou shalt not steal" I didn't see anyone looking guilty in the congregation. It was only when I got to the seventh I suddenly remembered where I'd left my bike.'

Now the clanger in this little story is that (as many readers of this book will know) the commandment that undoubtedly jogged the young vicar's memory comes *before* 'thou shalt not steal' – so the story falters by this simple inaccuracy. Does such a small error matter in what is only a story told for fun? If retaining credibility as a writer is important, it does.

Newspapers are not joke books or collections of funny stories but humour is *always* wanted in one form or another. It's easy to laugh at humour, not easy to write it and virtually impossible to teach someone how to do it. Lucky you if you know how.

4. Style

'He writes with such style,' glowed a popular columnist's admirer. All I really understand from such a remark is that the speaker enjoys reading work written with what he calls style. What style *is* – in that sense – I don't know. I do know that thought must be structured before writing can be, and that there is a deal of nonsense written and spoken about style. 'Good taste' is similarly vague and entirely subjective. Several long-time journalists claim that what are now called 'media studies' are threatening to push aside real journalistic values and skills in teaching colleges – and that too much lofty talk about 'style' has reduced it to a word that means nothing. As certainly as what appears to me to be in good taste may not appeal to you at all, so what is one man's (or woman's) style is another's poison.

Call it what we may, this chapter is about how to approach the task of turning a few random thoughts or ideas in one's head, or something even vaguer than that perhaps, into perfect finished copy pristine on white A4 paper ready for dispatch.

Imagine you've selected your subject, your special slant on it, what it's going to make (letter, feature, etc.) in which market, and you're ready to start writing. Or are you? One school of thought says, at this point, 'Write it down. You can always mess it about later, but until it's there in front of you it doesn't exist.' That is not bad advice, but there can be a clinging permanency about those first efforts, particularly when you may not yet possess the boldness to cut and prune what you've written. On the other hand, you may opt for not committing anything definite to paper for the moment while you think further about what your plan is and just how you are going to write it. Let's see what we can learn from people in earlier times.

Our language has developed through centuries of being spoken rather than written – before the mass of ordinary people learned to read – and spoken words are constantly changing in use and meaning. Words written as they are spoken in casual speech are not hard to find in print and even in public places. I regularly pass a road sign directing folk to the local 'Libary'; elsewhere a notice at a pet rescue centre announces the services of a 'Vetinary surgeon'.

The purpose of writing is to communicate, yet today the 7th-century Old English of Caedmon, England's earliest known poet, is almost completely unreadable and seems to be unrelated to our present usage. After the Normans our language evolved to what we called Middle English, and the words of Chaucer (1340–1400) are quite recognisable although the spelling seems odd to us. The 16th-century English of Tyndale's translation of the Bible became the language of Jane Austen (d. 1817) whose English is hardly distinguishable from the tongue we use today.

Dr Johnson's dictionary, not the first but the most successful in the mid-18th century, was also published in weekly parts at sixpence each, so it must have reached a wide audience. Earlier attempts at creating a standard English had met with much argument and opposition, and by this time informal standards already existed to register the meaning of legal, government and trade documentation. By its very nature evolution is continuous and standards change. You cannot freeze the language at some point and decry any future variations. For this reason no dictionary, however august, is entirely 'correct'. Even within British English the concept of correctness is not one favoured by language scholars. 'Accepted usage' is about the closest they allow and even then the population referred to must be defined. What is accepted usage to a group of Army officers may not be so to a group of taxi-drivers – and vice versa. The best that dictionaries can do is to reflect common usage.

Neither, for the same reason, is there any spelling authority for all time except perhaps for those in the legal profession. If the 'z' disappears from English (although with the American insistence on 'ize' ending so many good English words closing with 'ise' this seems unlikely to happen) it will be following letters like the Middle English letter for 'th', which changed to look like a 'y' for a while (hence 'Ye') before being replaced by a separate 't' and 'h' ('Thee'). There were in fact two such characters: one to represent the soft 'th' sound as in 'thought' and the other for the hard sound as in 'though'. Incidentally, when Noah Webster published his first American Dictionary (about fifty years after Johnson) its decisions on spelling were greeted with much mocking from this side of the pond. Some so-called 'Americanisms' in common use today lead to unexpected results. One is the habit of replacing 'Have you got?' with 'Do you have?' 'Do you have children?' a US gynaecologist asked a woman. 'Yes,' she replied, 'About every other year.'

In truth many words and spellings of words that we think of as American (like 'gotten') are in fact old English. It's we who have changed. 'Gotten' was almost entirely out of use in the educated world when we were settling the Americas. But one little girl in Wigan cares naught for the scholars and pundits on either side of the Atlantic. 'He's got it wrong,' she corrected a fellow pupil in her class. 'He's gone and put "putten" when he should have putten "put".'

There has never been one English language. English differs by region and educational background within the UK; accent, grammar and vocabulary all play a part in making ours the richest and most 'stylish' in the world.

How are you going to use it?

Being practical

We'll imagine you live near Hampton Court in West London and plan to write an article for your local evening paper about the reinvigoration of the famous Hampton Court maze. After more than three hundred years the maze is to be entirely replanted, as it has become so threadbare it no longer poses a challenge to its half-million annual visitors from all over the world. Details of the plans have not yet been officially released, but you have managed to pull a few strings and feel that both revelations of what is afoot and a survey of earlier attempts at revitalisation of the maze (in the 1960s it was badly patched up with yew trees planted too closely together) would be of great interest to local readers. Your research has been thorough and you are confident you have plenty of material. This is a good place to remind you that stubborn determination to use every scrap of research material you have unearthed, relevant or not, can ruin a good feature. Don't feel you've been working to no purpose and wasting your time if you can't or don't use it all. In any case, you will (I hope) keep everything you've found. Its value in the future will more than reward you for any restraint this first article might require. Never content yourself with writing just one or two pieces about a topic when your research could keep you funded to sell to local papers, freesheets, regional, trade and maybe daily papers as well. I confess the only hardship I find in wringing research dry is that I get tired of the subject. I can be sure my readers won't, because they are never the same people reading the same thing, and of course each article is different from the others.

Or let's assume you are equally optimistic about a different choice of market, the regional daily in your area, for another story. You have delved back into the old days when what is now a local cinema was a theatre and music hall. Many old-time stars appeared there and had lodgings in the town at the time. You've dug deeper and found several of the families (or their offspring) in whose homes the stars lodged, perhaps even a few still living in the same houses. Some of the many people who worked in the old place in its heyday are delighted to share their recollections with you – and readers – and your research file is bulging with fascinating material. This is just an example of the type of article you might be planning, but it could be something quite different. A report on your trek across South America, facts and figures about women's clubs, keeping your teeth in good condition, the incidence of broken marriages among servicemen and women overseas, the history of old coins unearthed in your area – no matter what your topic, it is essential to have done your homework before you start writing.

Having said that, I remember a well-established writer friend who prefers to research a little to give himself the feel of what he's doing, then write his piece, leaving little gaps where he knows he needs to do more research, and fill the gaps later. It works very well for him and perhaps it would for you. But don't let this method of working be an excuse for not getting down to the research properly or for skimming over the surface of your topic. Recalling my colleague's way of working and how I almost dismissed it as unworkable illustrates two important points: that it is unwise to be dogmatic about such a wild, wanton and wholly personal thing as writing and that, in writing, there is no inflexible rule about anything.

Say you've been in contact with the paper's features editor who has shown interest in the subject and has asked to see what you have to offer – albeit without any firm commitment. He might have suggested they will arrange pictures (unless you can do so yourself) and you know the length you will be writing to. You are very familiar with the paper, reading it almost every day, and in your mind's eye you can see your feature having a good spread. You can almost hear and see the ensuing lively and appreciative comment from nostalgic readers and you are mentally spending the good fee you have negotiated (you have discussed that with the paper, haven't you?).

At last you feel you are ready to write your rough draft. There's no need to start at the beginning for you can be happily uninhibited, knowing no eyes but yours will ever see your initial efforts. At this early stage you might take one or more sheets of rough A4 paper (the backs of other unwanted sheets) and sketch out a crude shape to the piece: a title, a strong intro (first par), a possible order of the main points of the article, a neat ending. Then what? Write it up? Er, *how?*

You could open with a bit of explanation about the story and why you're telling it, continue in a straightforward narrative about the history of the theatre and embark on a more-or-less chronological progress through its fortunes and failures, ending with some regrets about its impending demolition. Follow that unimaginative and wholly predictable recipe with no other ingredients and you could make it acceptable (if the editor were desperate or not feeling very well), but you are more likely to make it ploddingly boring. The article – any article and every piece of writing of any sort – needs lift and buoyancy, or what the advertising men call 'oomph' or 'zizz', to make it different and (more importantly) irresistible. What it needs is *style*.

For want of a better word

Are we going round in circles in echoing the word 'style' as used by my young friend in the first paragraph of this chapter? No. In my book, *this* book, style is an amalgam of many attributes, all of them relating as much to the writer as to what is written. There are writers who insist that attempting to dissect style is to kill it and that if it does not come naturally, too bad; maybe you'll get better one day. That's not my view. If I can reduce a problem into manageable portions I improve my chances of getting to grips with it. Consider this apparent paradox: your best style is what is naturally 'you': any accomplished writer can write in several styles. I believe the former statement applies at the start of one's writing career, the latter is certainly true with greater experience. Even then your style is as much 'you' as are your voice, your mannerisms and the way you walk; it cannot be otherwise. You can adapt your writing style as you wish, although just now we are discussing style in the light of a definite market, a considered and researched topic, and the slant chosen for it. To a large degree these points will determine the writing style.

But there is more to it than that. I've narrowed down what I think style means (although other writers may disagree with me, for style, like beauty, is in the eye of the beholder) and I here offer as simple a distillation of it as I can. With everything I write my hope is to let the following factors loiter in the subconscious and trust they will weave some sort of spell. Occasionally they do; often they won't. I list them here in no order of priority except for the first which – to my mind – is paramount.

Clarity

Everything we write must be plain, unambiguous and relevant. Excessive jargon and poor grammatical construction cloud good writing. That means we want the active voice, positive words and no long meandering sentences. If we don't make what we are trying to say crystal clear, we might as well not bother to write it down.

'Girls now smoke more cigarettes than boys.' Oh, so girls have taken to smoking boys, have they?

'Peter met his brother at the station. He had been working all day.' Who had been working all day?

'Peter met his brother at the station after working all day' makes it Peter. 'Peter met his brother at the station and thought how tired he looked after working all day' makes it the brother.

'The natives looked friendly but they didn't offer them any food.' Who didn't offer any food and who didn't get any? 'The natives looked friendly but didn't offer the travellers any food' or 'The natives looked friendly but the travellers didn't offer them any food' makes it plain who went hungry.

It is so easy, fatally easy, to assume readers will understand what we writers don't even recognise as a possible cause of mis-understanding.

Accuracy

If clarity begins at home, so does accuracy. This means not only getting the facts right, important as that is, but also being accurate about how they sit on the page. Inaccuracy has two common causes, one of which is faulty sentence construction. I saw this in a national paper that ought to hang its head in shame: 'Standing on the bridge the National Theatre is an impressive sight.'

Can't you picture foreign tourists or folk who have no knowledge of London reading that and thinking, 'We must go and see that theatre built on a bridge!' Of course the National Theatre does not stand on any bridge, so our tourist friends are in for a disappointment. What the writer meant (but didn't think it necessary to say) was, 'The National Theatre is an impressive sight seen from the bridge' or 'When you stand on the bridge . . .'.

Another newspaper item said: 'At the age of three her father took her to Canada.' Advanced, wasn't he, for a three-year-old?

The other common cause of inaccuracy is using a word or phrase you think is the one you want when it isn't. And I'm not referring to genuine mistakes like the one a writer made in referring to her word-processor as a 'word-suppressor' or the obituary of a distinguished General which referred to him as 'battle-scared' with an unfortunate omission of a second 'r' in 'scared'. (To make matters worse, the paper printed a correction the next day which described the General as 'bottle-scarred'.) Nor do I mean unintentional howlers such as, 'When a new burial ground is developed, a number of bodies start to take an interest' (from the *Kingston Guardian*).

At a time when interest rates had risen from 5.25 per cent to 6.25 per cent a national paper reported, 'Interest rates have risen by 1 per cent.' In fact a rise of 1 per cent would take 5.25 per cent to 5.3025 per cent and what should have been reported was that rates had risen by one percentage *point.*

'Borrow' and 'lend' may be no problem but are you happy about 'infer' and 'imply', or 'principle' and 'principal', 'agoraphobia' and 'acrophobia'? What determines whether you use 'after' or 'afterwards'? I think it downright sneaky, by the way, for 'invalid' to be the reverse of 'valid' when 'invaluable' is not the reverse of 'valuable'.

What about 'fewer' and 'less'? (If you're wondering, 'fewer' can be counted but 'less' can't.) Are you a sucker for phrases like 'expeditiously effected an exit' (left quickly)? Do you write redundant words: 'She filled up the kettle', or 'There was more to follow later'? Are you guilty of 'different to' or 'fed up of'?

Accuracy insists we must not write unthinkingly, but our mistakes do not occur to most of us until they are brought to our attention by someone else.

Listen to people talking and you will often hear words used incorrectly; we are all guilty at times. Adverbs used with discretion can greatly enhance writing but they are often superfluous; for example, 'the leaf fluttered gently': how else does anything flutter? 'Hopefully' is a word that may alter the interpretation of a sentence without the speaker being aware of it. 'The bypass will be completed next year' is a bald statement. 'Hopefully the bypass will be completed next year' immediately reveals a personal view. People living in houses bordering the bypass might not agree; 'regrettably' could reflect their feelings more accurately. This objection apart, 'hopefully' is an adverb – a word added to a verb to express a modification of it. Is a bypass capable of hope, or regret? Following the current trend in talking is not necessarily the best way to write for papers of any level. We don't want to talk like textbooks on English grammar and we all know speech has a brief life. But put any solecism, however minor, in writing and you bestow on it a credibility it doesn't deserve.

While appreciating the importance of keeping abreast of modern thought and idiom, how are your clichés? Phrases and sayings are sharp and appropriate the first time round, not so endearing when you've heard them a few times, and a bore when you find them at every turn. So today's clichés may be tomorrow's groans. There's nothing new under the sun? Perhaps, for I thought 'In this office, clichés will be avoided like the plague' very amusing when I saw it on the wall of a newspaper office. People around me sighed; I should at least have noticed the cutting was going brown at the edges. Stereotyped writing is another hazard. Do you use phrases that should have lain down and died years ago? (Are you happy that 'lain' is the right word here or do you suspect it should be 'laid'?)

Newspapers use adjectives only when they have a definite purpose on the page. Avoid clichéd, meaningless double adjectives ('full unabridged' story, 'great big' ball) as adjectives should extend nouns, not prop them up. They should inform or describe but never make the reader stop with a query. 'Long' doesn't tell him how long; 'short' is how short? And there are pairs of words that are not interchangeable, although most of us are not sure which to use where. Like these:

'The cake that my mother baked for me was delicious.'
'The cake which my mother baked for me was delicious.'

Which is correct? Hands up who chose the second? Good. The reasoning behind the distinction is this: 'that' defines and 'which' informs. This is an over-simplification for the sake of clarity; in truth both sentences would be better without that or which at all. The point is that in the first sentence 'that' assumes readers already know my mother baked the cake and I am simply referring to it again so they will know which particular cake I'm talking about. In the second sentence, 'which' introduces new information about the cake regardless of whether or not readers have already heard about it. As for any commas there might or might not be in these sentences – read on.

The problem of 'he or she', 'him or her', and so on, constantly crops up as a thorn in newspaper copy. What do you think of this? 'I like Wensleydale cheese. But everyone to his or her favourite.' What an artificial and grammatically correct second sentence. Does anybody like the taste of that? Melting down the cheese is the only solution. Using plurals is one way of recasting the sentence: 'people have their favourites'. Avoiding the use of 'his or her' is another: 'everyone has a favourite'. 'We all have our favourites' is a third and the one I would choose, partly because it flows more easily in print but chiefly because the 'we' puts me on the same level as the reader and everything I write should be viewed through his (her *sic*) eyes and not mine. Using the first person plural gives this 'one of us' feeling quite naturally. Contrast such usage with 'It is thought' or 'It is said' (by whom, anyway?), which is totally impersonal. In quality papers in the right circumstances, fine; in lighter vein it drives a ditch between you and your readers – and why should they bother to jump over it?

Euphony

Euphony is a funny thing. You only think about it when it isn't there. A piece of written work, be it a news story, an article, a Letter to the Editor or even a filler, consists of silent words on paper, but take them all together and there is – or should be – a rhythm, a satisfaction, a *something* that leaves the reader feeling at the end, 'Yes, that was well written.' You think this is pretentious talk that would be scorned by your local paper or freesheet? Not at all. As children learning to read we hear the words in our heads and at an early age we say them aloud. With maturity comes that curious state of absorbing what we read without being aware of it; we no longer read individual words strung together but whole pieces of written work. Indeed so strong is this absorption concept that it is almost impossible not to use it; showing cards to prisoners for two seconds announcing their imminent execution, in a language they deny knowing, is considered a sophisticated and effective form of torture in some repressive regimes.

We writers refer to the 'flow of writing' or 'being in full flow' and perhaps when that is happening the euphony factor is taking over subconsciously exactly as we want it to. It's easy to spoil it, to 'lose the flow', as we all know. Using a muddled phrase, getting facts wrong, chasing up a blind alley and then trying to write our way out of trouble – all these can break the euphony. So can a sudden unwarranted switch in viewpoint or tense, a misplaced adverb or an inconsistency in mood. In practical terms, inadequate attention to structure, paragraph size and punctuation can jar readers out of sympathy in a trice. When that happens they immediately lose their absorption capacity. Euphony gives way to exasperation. They may start reading the paragraph or sentence again with jaded interest all too easily abandoned, or they may not bother . . .

We tend to talk in longer sentences than we use when writing because speech is so much more rapid. It can be a surprise to count the number of words most newspapers use 'in one breath'. Seven or eight is not abnormal for a sentence in the tabloids, especially in that important opening sentence. For a proper assessment and to satisfy your market's requirements it is worth studying a paper's density, sometimes called the 'fog index'. This is a practical formula for working out how easy or difficult the writing is to read and understand. The use of long or unusual words and convoluted sentences slows down the natural absorption of information. Make the fog level match the readers' educational level, goes the argument, and communication will be effortless.

Work it out like this: from the paper take any extract of 100 words (give or take one or two) finishing at the end of a sentence. Count the number of sentences in that extract and divide 100 by that number. This gives you the average length of the sentences in the extract. Now count the number of words of

more than two syllables and add that figure to the average
sentence length. Halve the result and you have the paper's
density. Here is an example:

Number of sentences in extract = 9
100 divided by 9 = 11 (say) which is the average sentence
    length
Words of more than 2 syllables = 25
11 + 25 = 36
Half 36 = 18 which is the paper's density.

Because the number of words of more than two syllables is part
of the formula for establishing the density of a paper, the result
will also indicate the simplicity or difficulty of its words compared to other papers. Now try it with any extract of your own
work. A fog level of between 8 and 12 generally suits copy for
readers up to GCSE standard and is considered the normal level
for popular journalism. For the general population this is also
thought to be the most comfortable level, unflattering as that
may seem. University or postgraduate levels of 'fog' may reach
up to 18, but it may be better to rewrite anything registering a
level higher than this. This is definitely a situation where more
fog means less clarity.

To establish and maintain euphony, vary sentence length
even within the paper's density. And don't forget sentences of
one or two words or without verbs have a valid place; we are
talking to people in their own language, not writing a postgraduate thesis. Variety of construction is important, too, lest
we drone and bore. An adjectival phrase, for instance, can be a
useful opener for the occasional sentence but is an irritant if
used to excess. Here's an overdose:

'Wanting to catch the train, Jack rushed across to his car.
Trusting traffic would be light that morning . . . Thinking the
office might be closed and fearing he would be too late . . .
Worried he might not have another chance . . .'

Could you bear much more of that?

Alliteration has its place but the pages of newspapers may
not be where you'll find much of it, except, perhaps, in
specialised feature material – and then sparingly.

Brevity

The 'soul of wit', as Shakespeare described brevity, is so important I would have placed it higher had I been establishing an
order of importance. Brevity doesn't mean, as I thought in my
youth, cut and cut and cut until only the bare bones of a piece
remain (sometimes there was nothing left by the time I'd
finished). Nor, of course, is it only writing short pieces ('Oh
good,' think the ingenuous, 'that's easy'). Brevity means telling
in 300 words a story you've first written in 400, leaving out
nothing that matters. Call it conciseness or economy instead if
you prefer; it is the essence of good writing and a skill learned
by constant observation and practice. See how you score by
writing a piece and then rewriting it more tightly, or by trying
to improve on what someone else has written, always remem-
bering the criterion of not cutting out anything important.

As an aid to brevity I recommend making sure a high proportion of your writing sticks firmly to the point. Rough judgement about how well it does this is hardly enough as you skim
through the completed draft. Count the words that truly relate
to the topic; the number will depend on what the topic is and
your slant on it, but the higher the proportion of relevant words
and phrases the tighter your copy will be.

Train yourself to start at the beginning. This is not as foolish
as it may sound, for beginners often meander round the edge of
a story before getting to its nuts and bolts. Opening sentences
must be brief, accurate and attention-grabbing – so make sure
there are no sub-clauses wandering about here. But stamp your
individuality on your work from the beginning (you will hardly
be able to do otherwise). For a good start don't be afraid to use
the unexpected and be wary of using quotations; many are
hackneyed or boring.

The ideal first par homes in on one idea, scene or propo-
sition, making your first image as clear in the readers' heads as
a television picture or photo. So that first sentence bears a
heavy burden. Is it about the story you are going to unfold,
explaining how you come to be writing it or why it is such a
tricky subject to write about? If it is, delete it. A fair test is to
put the story aside for a few days so you can come to it with a
sharper critical sense and then start reading it from the third or
even the fourth paragraph. If you realise that is where the story
really begins, cut out those waffly ones that came first.

Words and phrases that don't work for a living are wimps and have no place in newspaper copy. Eliminating them is another way to tighter writing. Spot the wimps in this:

The villages are quite large and a good number of the people live by fishing and a spot of hunting. Their huts are very small and very overcrowded, especially when three or more generations manage to live together under one roof.

'Quite large' and 'very small' mean nothing without a yardstick. Is a cat quite large to a mouse or an elephant? Are beans very small compared to apples or grains of rice? How many people is 'a good number'? And what about a 'spot of hunting'? 'Very' is vague and I can't think how people of any age range could live together and not be 'under one roof'.

Writing with brevity is nothing more than stepping back, taking a hard look at what you've written and being ruthless when you need to be. Long-windedness, repetition without cause, talking off the subject, vagueness, dragging, and not knowing where the article is going are slicing points. But you'll save yourself time, of course, if you learn to write with brevity in the first place.

Magic

Writing for newspapers is, as I stress, practical and functional. There is little room for what is commonly termed the 'art' of writing, although perhaps the process of writing what is wanted clearly and simply is itself an art. Despite this no-nonsense approach, the best newspaper writers manage – at the right moment, according to what they're writing – to lift readers above the story, to give them a sudden glow or to lighten what might be a black period in their lives. It is done in several ways, and if these include the use of carefully selected artifice the effect is no less heart-warming.

Writing of every sort is partly artifice, when all's said and done, although there are still some folk who imagine that if it doesn't come without effort you're not a writer. Artifice has a poor reputation because it sounds deceitful and 'on the make', but I use the term here with readers' best interests in mind. Artifice is only permissible when used with depth and honesty. Figures of speech and emotive words with special impact are examples of the use of artifice, and they can make a happy incident linger in a reader's memory where bald narrative might not; touching a nostalgic or deeply buried chord may raise a childlike wonder and optimism not experienced for years. If they are relevant to a story, expressing your own emotions – not in sickly sentimentality nor tongue-in-cheek and certainly never in excess – can let readers know somebody cares and that they're not alone in their troubles. The 'magic' factor can draw from readers that contented sigh we all want to hear, 'Ah, that's good.'

Clarity, euphony, brevity: three basic platforms on which to build.

House style

A newspaper's 'house style' is very different from the style we've been talking about. Observing the house style means following established rules and customs in punctuation, paragraphing, the use of capital letters and hyphens, the precise way of writing numbers, dates, abbreviations and everything else that has to be set in text. As your copy will be set in columns, go easy on the dashes; they can make newspaper columns look gappy and unkempt. William Rees-Mogg, when editor of *The Times*, put in the style book a prohibition on any sentence longer than 12 words. Whatever the house rules are, they exist only for the convenience of everyone writing for the paper (no more uncertainty about whether to give them '1, 2, 3' or 'one, two, three', and so on) and for consistency. It would look ill-organised to print 'Doctor F Higgins Jones' in one par and refer to him lower down the page as 'Dr. F. Jones', or to print 'etcetera' on page 2 and 'etc.' on page 4. The latter raises a typical house style problem: 'etcetera' is, I think, unique in being spoken in full but commonly written in abbreviated form. In its shortened form, does 'etc.' have a full stop after it when it's in the middle of a sentence, only at the end of a sentence, in both situations or in neither? The house style will supply the answer.

Inconsistencies can leap off the printed page and detract from the story. Pointing out such irregularities was a favourite topic for Letters to the Editor before the introduction of house style books. Nowadays these tend to lie around offices getting dirty and lost; if you can't get hold of one (and a request may be treated with bemused astonishment), I suggest you make your own by keeping an eye on the newspaper of your choice and making a note of any quirkiness that may trip you up.

Scaffolding and construction

If the reader has to adjust his interpretation of what he's reading halfway through (and go back and start again if he's sufficiently interested), there's something seriously wrong with it. Capricious scaffolding could be the weakness. Only the designer knows it was there; it was the only structure that held the whole edifice together at the beginning, and nothing could have been built at all without it. A writer is the designer and the builder, but first he has to erect the scaffolding – and make sure it is strong.

Broadly speaking, a piece of work (other than the briefest) is shaped into paragraphs. They are not chunks of prose cut at random, for paragraphing has a definite purpose. It breaks up copy to make it more attractive to read; a large slab of print is a deterrent to the casual reader and if he skips past your article without sampling it he won't know whether he likes the taste. A paragraph talks about one aspect of your main topic (just as a sentence has a single thought) and when you've finished with that aspect it is time to move on to the next par with the next point you wish to make. If what you want to say is going to take a lot of space, making too long a par for comfort, simply break it up into two or more. There's no rule that says you must contain all you want to say at that moment in a single par. It is more important not to deter a reader with an indigestible block of words. As with sentences, varying the length of paragraphs makes for a lighter and more easily swallowed article.

Variety in paragraph construction is also important in making the written piece easy on the eye and effortless to take into the head. The first par or intro of any piece has a particular job: to keep people reading. People don't read papers in the same way as they might read fiction. They could be reading a newspaper while standing at a bus stop or taking a quick coffee break, and the story in front of them cannot afford a leisurely beginning. Intros, therefore, must get to the point at once, besides being simple and capable of being instantly absorbed. I find my best ones when I'm not sitting at my desk, but perhaps driving or in the bath. Being denied the help of a scribbling pad forces me to an intro that is vivid and brief – otherwise I'll forget it before I can write it down. Later I find it often says just what I want it to say.

Just as starting too many sentences with an adjectival phrase can be irritating, so the involuntary repetition of a particular 'shape' can make one par look like another regardless of its content. Read a feature in a quality daily or regional paper and notice how adopting a different strategy for each par avoids giving readers the same doorstep to climb over and over again. If you find it hard to identify different paragraph shapes, listen to the radio and imagine you have to present a report about – say – whaling in Alaska in written form. As you listen, think where you would end one par and open a new one. And here's another tip.

To build the written piece one paragraph has to follow its predecessor smoothly; it needs a 'joiner'. A newspaper writer knows he must keep readers reading and that means keeping them sufficiently interested to bridge the mental jump of eye and brain from one par to the next. That's hardly a difficult jump, you could be thinking. But drifting to another item on the page is sometimes easier. So we use a technique to keep them reading by leaving a little 'come-on' dangling at the end of a paragraph. Go back to the last par, which ends with the short sentence 'And here's another tip.' This is a 'come-on' to entice you into reading the following par (although this device is less appropriate in books and I use it here merely to illustrate a technique). A good public speaker will use the same device before pausing to take a sip of water, to deter folk in the audience from using the break to make a rush for the exit.

Paragraph joiners may be phrases or single words, and you can spot them at the start of many a good par. Out of place, they can make your pars overdressed; 'moreover', 'nevertheless' and 'notwithstanding' make the less portentous 'however' more acceptable, although even that is hardly the normal parlance of tabloid readers. 'All the same' and 'even so' are more comfortable, but – as always – the market is king. 'Yet', 'but', 'despite', and conjunctions of time like 'when' come naturally. And there's nothing amiss about joining with 'and', hesitant as you might be to make your old schoolteacher flinch.

Many joiners serve more than the purpose of linking one par to the previous one. As 'and' continues with what you're saying, 'for' introduces a reason, a result, or a new development, 'so' is tantamount to saying 'and the consequence is, or was' and 'but' involves a stepping back and looking at the matter from the other side. 'Now' can be patronising and should be used with care. It may be a complacent pause by a writer more fascinated by what he's writing than is good for him; usually what it says is 'at last we're getting to the point of this story'.

The topic and slant will determine the tenor of the pars you write, and a news story, for example, will be written more crisply than a feature. Whatever the piece, does narration tell the story effectively or is exposition more appropriate? The active voice (being more positive and immediate) is usually better in news stories than the passive, but all paragraphs, as all sentences and even all words, must keep the story moving. Being specific is better than being general and plain words are often best. 'Said' and 'began' are easier on the inward ear than 'responded' and 'commenced'. Write as readers talk and choose shorter words in place of phrases: 'because' not 'due to the fact that', 'saw' not 'observed', and 'now' instead of the ghastly 'at this moment in time'.

It must be the ease with which punctuation is sprinkled about that makes it so tempting, but it is best used with restraint. Its *raison d'être* is two-fold: to facilitate smooth reading and to ensure what has been written is not misunderstood. In its latter capacity it guards against ambiguity. If you don't know your colon from your inverted commas, your punctuation could be doing quite the reverse. We need to know the function of the different punctuation marks and where they should be placed. All emphasis is no emphasis and to overdo punctuation is a mistake. Be particularly careful in the use of exclamation marks, which are usually unnecessary and undesirable. Too often they mean 'see how clever I am!!!' Fashions come and go even in punctuation. At one time the accepted format for 'one, two, and three' was to insert a comma before 'and'. Now that extra comma (known as the 'Oxford comma' from its popularity with the Oxford University Press) is usually discarded. But there is still a need for it at times; consider 'shopping in Marks and Spencers and Woolworths'. Anyone familiar with shopping would almost certainly know how many shops were visited. A stranger, if asked, might reply, 'Three.'

Are you in need of a brush-up on what you learned at school or can't remember learning? Can you identify a synonym? Do you know when to use 'shall' or 'will'? Can you tell a transitive verb from an intransitive one? Do you know what a collective noun is? Take a few hours a week (or even a few minutes a day) to browse through *The Macmillan Good English Handbook* by Godfrey Howard which is packed with rules, recommendations, options and cautions in a unique at-a-glance format (see also Chapter 6: Research and Help).

Observing the rules of basic grammar is no more than acquiring the ability to write good English. I hope the confusion that can occur when folk who consider grammar and punctuation beneath them have their way is enough to convince wavering readers of its importance. Consider this: 'The boys, who arrived too late, found all the tickets had been sold.' Both those commas should be omitted. A comma works hard in its role of providing a breathing space for the reader, but this sentence is short enough not to need one. Note the difference between a subsidiary clause that *defines* (contributing information of substance) and one that *describes* (merely adding information). Not sure which is which? If it can be left out without hurting the sentence, it's descriptive. There are instances where this test doesn't apply but they are rare. Defining clauses hate being fenced off between commas. In the sentence quoted above 'who arrived too late' is plainly definitive as it explains why they didn't get any tickets. More subtly, sandwiching 'who arrived too late' between commas bestows it with less significance than what you imply is to follow. As that is not the case here, the reader is left with a whiff of dissatisfaction.

Changing the sentence to 'The boys, who were wearing green shirts, found . . .' makes the subsidiary clause descriptive; it adds information by telling us the colour of the boys' shirts. Apply the test. The commas should be left in place. You disagree? Cut them out, then, and we're left with 'The boys who were wearing green shirts found all the tickets had been sold.' Ah, readers not party to this discussion might think, so boys in red or yellow or blue shirts got tickets but the organisers refused to sell any to green shirt-wearers. No, that's not what we mean, is it? There must be something in this punctuation business after all; it's not just pedantic nonsense.

Alas, writing good English and punctuating it well is one thing, but writing for newspapers can be rather different. Only you can decide which markets to write for and what work you do. Should you ever feel disheartened about standards, remember there are papers to satisfy everybody, and no matter which you choose, you must put yourself in the place of their readers if you wish to sell.

Professional journalists use countless tricks of the trade every day: implying something without actually saying it, repetition for a particular reason, slowing up or quickening pace, deliberate facetiousness, compression for a special effect. All these techniques give impact and colour. Read papers with a new eye and you can't help but learn more. And when your copy is published always compare it with what you put in, and learn from the difference.

At last your piece is done – almost. How do you end it? This is called 'casting off'. Its prime demand is urgency; when you've finished, *finish*. If you meander on with extra thoughts you should have inserted earlier or ones that don't belong in the story, a sub-editor will cast off for you. Then it may not be a cast-off so much as a cut-off, which is usually as unsatisfactory an experience as is its verbal cousin on the telephone. Casting off simply means ending the story succinctly and at the right time. Cutting off is what the sub-editor does when the copy overruns. It is either too long for the space allotted or, more probably, it doesn't end at the end of the story. Woe to the writer whose work is cut off. If you have saved your *pièce de résistance* till last it's likely to suffer a *coup de grâce*.

News stories

When you've heard half a dozen eye witnesses describe what happened at the scene of an accident, you begin to wonder about history. Plainly what is a fact to me may not always be the same to you, and your account of an event you saw may not tally with the one the man next door insists is right. How do we straighten out this apparent riddle?

Report a news story and what you'll be listening to at any one time is one person's opinion, although the speaker is convinced what he is saying is 'fact'. He's not lying (probably) but he may still be wrong; what he's telling you may not be fact at all. That is just one reason why news stories are tricky to write. It is important to seek 'facts' from as many people on the scene as you can.

There's another reason why a news story needs to be written with special care; we're back to the cutting off, which can inflict a mortal wound. The accepted method is to make it a pyramid. Let us say we have a story about a 12-year-old boy who was taken to a local maternity home to have his tonsils out; a fun story to write and one offering plenty of scope in a jokey style. If we were telling this innocuous tale to a friend we would enjoy building it up and keeping the punch-line – the boy's destination – to the end. Try that format as a newspaper piece and the end may never be printed at all.

Excessive length or overwriting is the usual reason for a cut-off, but it may not always be the writer's fault. There might be a change in the page layout for all sorts of reasons and no way can the freelance writer anticipate a shortage of space for news. The safeguard, therefore, is to write a news story so that if anything's going to be cut it will only be subsidiary matter at the end. Like this:

```
                        *
            *point*                    par A
          *—explain—*                  par B
        *——more info——*                par C
      *———elaborate on it———*          par D
    *————————'smalls'————————*         par E
```

Remember those good old questions every journalist should ask on a news story? The pyramid uses them all. I like Rudyard Kipling's version:-

> I kept six honest serving men,
> They taught me all I knew,
> Their names are WHAT and WHY and WHEN,
> And HOW and WHERE and WHO.

You need to watch the length of each par (or you may defeat the whole purpose) but in shape and substance the story will follow the pyramid above. Paragraph A will be the nub of it, the point that makes it news. 'Twelve-year-old Matthew Smith thought he knew the facts of life until he had his tonsils out in a maternity home . . .' (continue as you wish, with the answers to the questions 'Who?' and 'What?'). Let an intro hold the main point but don't overcrowd it. Details of place or people are best in the second par unless they add to whatever is striking about the intro.

Par B allows you space to explain what you've already written in par A, this time having discovered more in answer, perhaps, to the questions 'Where?', 'When?' and 'Why?' But par B should not exceed par A in importance. Down to par C and room for further information, but only matter of less significance to the story as a whole. Then to par D, and here may come details that wouldn't be missed, perhaps answering the question 'How?'

Lastly comes poor par E, the fall guy. It should only carry the 'smalls', i.e. extra little bits you might still wish to use but which don't contribute to the news value of the story. That being so, should par E be there? Don't use smalls as an excuse to overwrite the story. An editor or sub-editor might not cut it; he might find it less trouble to spike it – which means it won't be used at all.

Letters to the Editor

Most newspapers print a letters column, or even a full page of them. This is a part of the paper that is widely read because it tends to reflect everyday issues of immediate interest to most of the paper's readers. You may think this type of writing is a waste of your efforts if you won't get paid for it, but think again. It is generally understood that some papers do not pay (although others do) but contributions to the letters page are always worth a writer's time and effort. They can be mulled over in your head at any odd moments, take only a few moments to jot down and not many more to lick into shape.

A good Letter to the Editor can persuade him to do something or to take a special interest in some event, or it may initiate news coverage of the points raised in it. Letters may reflect genuine wishes, nostalgia, observations, indignation, complaints and (less frequently) praise from the paper's ordinary readers. Many letters never see the dark of print. Excessive moaning and negative criticism are first in the waste-paper basket, although constructive argument on a topic already raised can make good reading. 'I can't agree with . . .' is quite welcome if followed by an addition to something already written about or bringing a new perspective to it. The height of your neighbour's sunflowers, the reason why buses don't run on time in your area, a useful tip for mothers with young babies in cold weather, your favourite recipe for lemon curd, why you fear for Anglo-Chinese relations in the light of current events or why a remand home should not be built near your town; controversy may be a successful ingredient, brevity *always* is and almost every topic written from almost every viewpoint is your stock in trade. But letters are not always as innocuous or spontaneous as they may seem to be.

One colleague of mine (I'll call him John) uses them like this: he remembers it is, for example, the anniversary of the date when a past monarch granted the freedom of the city to a tireless lady charity worker who is now in an old people's home.

The granting of such freedoms is noteworthy; John has made a study of them and has an article drafted on just this topic with special reference to the honour it brought the city umpteen years ago; he also has some pictures of the old lady, with cuttings of the city's evening paper at that time, celebrating the event. Were John to submit his article to the editor 'cold' it could well be ignored among the many current events the paper has to cover. But, he tells me, any good gardener prepares his soil to give his plants a better chance of blooming.

Before the anniversary John has in mind, a letter will arrive on the editor's desk. It shows a reader's pride in his city and reminds the editor of the royal visit in such-and-such a year. Apart from the facts it reveals, there will be two essential points about this letter: it will be sent at exactly the right time (dictated by the frequency of publication) and it will not be written by John. The timing must be precise so the editor may be sufficiently interested to start looking round for a feature on the subject, and as for the letter-writer – John has many friends and relations the other side of the city.

Dishonest, you say? He would laugh at such naiveté, vowing many a writer uses this way of arousing local interest, which is no more than people do when placing advertisements about forthcoming events. But there is a snag, whether John writes such a letter himself or gets someone else to write it for him: sometimes it not only works but works too well. It is important to get his article to the editor at the right time. Perhaps before it is accepted other eager readers will have taken up the topic and flooded the editor with letters about it. Those words 'This correspondence is now closed' may kill off the goose for the very writer who laid the golden egg. It could be that you (without any of John's guile) have also spotted in the Letters to the Editor a 'peg' for an article you have ready to submit. Quite innocently your enterprise may spoil John's little plan.

All Letters to the Editor should be brief and to the point, and the point should be made at the beginning rather than the middle or end. A sub-editor might be interrupted by someone calling, the telephone ringing or some other small distraction – and truncate your precious thoughts. Make each letter about a single point and, with perhaps fewer than fifty words to play with, get to it straight away.

It's not hard to see which of the following would stand the better chance of publication. This:

I like to see dogs running about by the river just as they did when I was a youngster, because it reminds me of a neighbour's old collie we often used to play with, me and my friends. It was a gentle dog, I remember, and really wouldn't hurt a fly, except that one day . . .

Or this:

A dog pulled me out of a river when I was five, so I can't criticise owners . . .

Use casual language, as if you are talking to a friend. Split your infinitives if you feel like it and write *won't* and *can't* rather than *will not* and *cannot* if it sounds natural to do so.

Letters columns or pages often get put to bed early in the life of the paper to get them out of the way and free the staff's attention for more topical matters. It pays (if not literally) to see yours arrive on the editor's desk as soon as he sits down to start assembling his next issue. For a weekly this will usually be the day after publication of the previous issue. Daily and evening papers naturally attract more letters, so although your chances of publication may seem higher, the reverse may be the case and it can be harder to aim your letter to a particular day or date. You can only hope for the best by writing a letter the editor simply cannot ignore despite the large pile already claiming his attention.

A word of warning: getting your letter published is fine; coping with some of the repercussions of its publication may not be so agreeable. A lot of letters pass without comment, except perhaps from your admiring family and friends, but if you have invited readers of the paper to respond to something (finding an old friend you've lost touch with, perhaps, supplying a recipe for loganberry wine or telling you where to buy clogs) don't be surprised if they do just what you've asked – in great numbers. You should be ready to reply to everybody who writes to you, and this can take more time and trouble than you bargained for.

Although Letters to the Editor are an important and valued part of the paper, it's not wise to telephone asking if they're going to print yours and if so please will they send you a free copy, or saying that you only want to know so you can tell all your friends to rush out and buy the paper. Don't fear, either, that you will be barred because you have had letters published in the same pages on other occasions; some writers become real characters whose opinions evoke more from others and are read with affection or scorn or amusement, so their latest contributions will be received with special pleasure. Avid writers cover many topics and just keep writing. So don't pester. It isn't that the editor doesn't care about you or that he doesn't welcome your letter, merely that he also has larger matters to work on.

Typed letters are preferred, although this is the one part of the paper where handwritten copy is acceptable; letters, after all, are invited from everyone and not everyone is expected to own or have access to a typewriter, let alone a word-processor. Nor is it necessary to send a stamped addressed envelope; you will be wasting money if you do, for no letters are returned. You have bought the paper, goes the thought, so you are entitled to give the editor your views just as he has the right to publish or ignore them.

Writing Letters to the Editor may fill odd moments or keep you writing in an otherwise blank spell. It can provide agreeable satisfaction when you turn to the Letters page in the paper and may put a few pounds in your pocket; it's certainly not to be sneezed at. What's more, have your letters published in newspapers and you'll be in the distinguished company of George Bernard Shaw, Arthur Conan Doyle, Graham Greene, Evelyn Waugh and Kingsley Amis, among other well-known writers, not forgetting Disgusted of Tunbridge Wells.

Talking about style shouldn't blind us to a matter of fact: to write for a newspaper you may have your head filled with ambition for the quality of what you write (indeed you must have that ambition), but there's only one place for your feet at all times: on the ground.

5. Interviewing

'I only have one chance,' wailed a young journalist on the way to interview an up-and-coming artist, 'and I'm terrified.'

Conducting an interview with someone whose story is wanted for publication may seem to be a daunting task but providing prior preparation is taken, it need not be so. Anyone with an unusual story to tell – a sporting champion, the author of a recent best-seller, a leading pop star or someone in the news for any other reason – is someone readers of newspapers want to know about. Hundreds of people would be thrilled to have the opportunity of talking to their favourite personalities, of sitting alone and uninterrupted with plenty of time to ask everything they want to know; think of yourself as the luckiest person in the world to be chosen to do this job and it will soon become a pleasure rather than an ordeal.

It is important to understand the difference between a published interview and a piece merely about a particular person. The latter, sometimes called a profile, may concentrate on a single individual but will take a broader view including, perhaps, details and information about the childhood, background and past history of the person being discussed, with the opportunity to write from a more detached standpoint. An interview, albeit with a similar background of research and investigation, is a one-to-one meeting; its product is a close, personal and highly original result of the meeting and the interviewer's interpretation of it.

Perhaps the first question to ask is not whether the person you are going to interview is right for the interview's market but whether you are the right person to conduct an interview. The best interviewers are not born but made. Above all they are good listeners. Have you the right personality? It takes special perceptiveness and a greater degree of shrewdness and sympathy than many people possess, plus a liberal dose of tact, discretion and the ability to remain silent when required. Being able to rely on your own judgement is also important and (luckily) this confidence in yourself grows with practice. What is more, with experience you'll find newspaper interviewing becomes fun rather than work. You meet so many fascinating people and, for a little time at least, enter a world that may be very different from your own, and which you might otherwise have no opportunity of sampling.

A good interview imparts information, preferably new information, about the interviewee to the readers; it is not just a question-and-answer session. 'What would I like to know about him?' is a good question to ask – and answer – yourself. That an interviewer must be keenly interested in the interviewee almost goes without saying, but plunge into it with insufficient thought and it may become a nightmare.

Practical considerations come first. How long is the interview to be? When? Where? Will there be accompanying pix taking some of 'your' space? Does the editor ask for a particular type of interview, or is it assumed you know the market and how to write for it?

The 'victim'

If we freelances are in the position of being able to choose whom to interview, it is not always wise to let our own preferences dictate to us. Many suitable people will not be well known in more than their immediate area, whereas an achievement of special interest or a personal story from an unknown person could make ideal material. In the first case the attraction will be the interviewee; in the second it will be his story. Either or both could be valid reasons for your choice and the ultimate question is: is it of sufficient interest to enough of the paper's readers for the editor to accept your idea? From your own point of view, if you are a beginner at the craft of interviewing and nervous at jumping your first hurdle, choosing a less well-known victim could be wise and give you confidence for the future.

Perhaps your potential interviewee is well known and an editor may know more about him/her than you do, in the early stages. He will certainly know (or can soon find out) if rival papers are planning a similar interview. It's possible your subject may not generate the publicity the paper needs for a particular sales target; there could already be an interview with him in the pipeline; he may have a reputation, unknown to you, of demanding fees or making impossible conditions and of being more trouble than he is worth. But when all bodes well and the interviewee is just right for the paper, an editor will be even more pleased if he can arrange prior publicity. Circulation, revenue and the paper's image will receive a welcome boost. This is one reason why most interviews are commissioned pieces.

It almost goes without saying that your research into your interviewee's background must be comprehensive and undertaken with persistence. Don't stop finding out all you can about him until you are fully satisfied there is nothing relevant left to discover. You will be held responsible, as a freelance, for the accuracy of any information that appears in print regarding your interviewee. We freelances must remember that the paper publishing our interviews may (or may not) check our facts but it is up to us, not the paper, to ensure everything contained in interviews is accurate.

When and where

Circumstances will dictate when you approach your interviewee for consent to the project. You may have enough time to make the agreement first, with date, hour and place all arranged, and then begin your preparatory work; or you may fear your interviewee will decline unless you can show some evidence of having done at least some of your homework at the first approach; only you can choose the most propitious time to make it. Whatever you decide, remember some folk will be scared at the very word 'interview' but could respond favourably if you were to ask if they would like to 'talk' to you for the paper. Explain who you are, which paper will be publishing your interview (or you hope will be publishing it, if you are not yet commissioned), why you want to talk to him, about what, and indicate that you will readily fit in with his plans concerning dates, times, the length of the interview and so on.

What if your potential interviewee declines? Only you can decide whether a refusal means he's just playing hard to get and will give in if you're more persistent, he's learned to be wary of newspaper journalists (yes, when a few behave despicably, as they do, we all suffer) or he genuinely does not want any publicity. In this tough and uncompromising world of newspapers some journalists will urge you to be ruthless, to ignore pleas for privacy and to hit hard if you want to succeed, regardless of other people's wishes. Maybe you can – and will. I can't.

It is important to opt for the best time and place for the interview (if you are in a position to choose), for both frequently affect the result. An interview over a meal is not to be recommended unless you are skilled at balancing plates with pens and notebooks, eating, drinking, asking questions and recording the answers all at the same time. Quiet country pubs may be good venues for seeing the interviewee loosen up and – perhaps – drop a few confidences, but the privacy of his house is likely to be a better venue. Accommodating the interviewee's wishes is kindly and could make him feel well disposed towards you, but meeting somewhere not likely to be disrupted by outside influences is more sensible. Combine the two for optimum effect.

Written consent is seldom necessary when someone agrees to be interviewed; if a person is in the public eye his secretary or manager will have a note of it, although you may like to confirm your part of the agreement in writing to ensure there are no mistakes regarding place, time, length of interview, likes and dislikes about voice recorders and so on. The less well known sometimes like to help with research in the interests of their own publicity; this is quite acceptable as long as there is no onus on you to feature any particular aspect of their lives or work. You hope you won't have to remind them of a simple fact – that the conduct of the interview is in your hands.

Part one – preparation

'*In partes tres divisa est,*' wrote Julius Caesar in his *Commentaries*. He was talking about Gaul, but might equally have been talking about the business of interviewing, for that is also divided into three parts: the preparation, the interview itself, and the work of writing it up afterwards. Preparation is like an iceberg in that nine-tenths will be hidden. It is often helpful to let a tenth show, for when you first approach your interviewee he will probably feel flattered on realising you have taken the trouble to do at least some outline homework about him. Later, during the course of the interview itself, the time and effort you have invested in preparation will prove its worth. So don't skimp on Gaul's first part; it may involve the most work but the more thoroughly it is done, the easier and more pleasant will be the interview that follows.

It is essential to familiarise yourself with your 'victim' so you don't waste time at the interview asking him questions to which you could well have found answers before you met. Unbeknown to him, therefore, you will have delved into his past. The more you find out about him, his background, family, career, likes, dislikes and anything else you can discover, the greater your confidence will be when you meet him face to face.

When planning an interview you will be able to use research material uniquely relevant to your interviewee. His friends working in his field of expertise, for example, with the same hobbies or shared experiences, may be able to give you information not to be found in any book. At the very least they will guide you on the vocabulary and basic knowledge of his special subject or achievement; without some grasp of what he may talk about you could soon get confused.

Cuttings already published about him will be valuable and may include previous interviews containing useful information. Perhaps he refers to a favourite sport or leisure occupation, or personal details may be revealed. Press releases may be available. Gather all information in your private notes regardless, at this stage, of how you might or might not make use of it. (Later, when you are more experienced in interviewing skills, you may have enough confidence to tackle the problem of selection as you do your research, but I do not advise such early restriction before you feel happy about it.) All your research and everything anybody tells you will provide you with a better basis for evaluation – and give you an increasingly logical perspective on the questions you may ask.

Before long it will be time to begin a rough plan of operation, but wait! The market – a newspaper – is the ruling hand in all your writing, and remains so in preparing for an interview. Your interviewee and the research you've uncovered will greatly influence the pattern you choose; interviews come in several styles like other writing. An old-fashioned formula is to compile questions more or less chronologically beginning with childhood and family life, then continuing with career-start and progress, problems, achievements and so on, according to what is relevant. This method still has its place as long as the pace doesn't drag (and it's difficult to prevent its doing so), but for many papers there is neither space nor reading time to tell the interviewee's whole story. The average reader's attention span is limited: if the first few words of the interview don't catch him, he'll turn his eyes elsewhere. Only your market will tell you how much of the whole you can cover and of prime consideration

___

will be whatever it is that makes your interviewee of interest to readers *at that time*. It may be a single aspect of his eventful life or an important piece of knowledge he can provide on a topical issue. Your thoughts on how to plan which questions to ask must be tempered by this restriction.

Generally it is not a good idea to ask anything controversial at the beginning. I usually work the plan into some sort of shape by writing down key questions as I think of them or as a particular item of research prompts me, on a large sheet of lined paper, leaving three or four lines between each question. This gives me room for more questions subsidiary to main ones or lets me chop and change my first thoughts as much as I need (and I always do). The flow of questions should vary in length, complexity and perhaps most of all in weight, with avoidance of any questions requiring only a 'yes' or 'no' response. Thoughtful and caring questions indicate your genuine interest in your interviewee and his theme, and encourage him to expand on what he really thinks and feels, which is just what you want to hear; a relaxed atmosphere leads him to speak more freely and informally. Ideally an interview should read like a spontaneous conversation. Questions that are predictable, dull or boring merely invite replies in the same vein. And they may bore your interviewee – with disastrous results.

If he is a well-known figure you may find a formidable amount of information about him, saddling you with a bundle of notes far too large to handle during the interview. You can't ask every question that occurs to you and selection raises its worrying head. Which aspects of his life or work can you safely omit? This is where a good memory, even a short-term one, is a blessing. Perhaps you, like me, daren't rely on it – so improvise with tiny *aides-mémoire* in your notes to jog you if the conversation wanders away from the track you've planned for it. Looking up some of my old notes for interviewing an elderly painter I find 'Somme' and 'Boots', which were enough to remind me he had lost the hearing in one ear on the Somme and was one of the first men to be fitted with an artificial hearing aid, and that he was a distant member of the family firm of the ubiquitous high street chemists.

When I've shaped my questions as I think best I write them out again and, if I'm relying on shorthand or written notes, I leave plenty of space after each question for the interviewee's reply. At an interview I also keep beside me a second sheet of paper reminding me about questions of lesser importance and this second sheet has an assurance value. I fancy I will remember the relevant basic facts about my man and they may not be directly referred to in the course of the interview, but if they are and I've forgotten – see my second sheet.

Part two – the interview

Knowing you've arrived (promptly) with the tools of the trade gives you confidence: a notebook, your prepared and/or semi-prepared questions, a pen or pencil (and a couple of spares) and your portable voice recorder if you plan to use one. There are many good models available, incidentally; not all are expensive or difficult to work, and using one will free you from having to take your eyes from your interviewee and his surroundings. Whatever machine you use, reliability is paramount or the entire interview could be lost. This is the sort of thing you might have nightmares about, but such anxieties are nothing to the horror that can happen when you're wide awake. You must be totally familiar with how your recorder works and how long the tape lasts, for any mid-interview fiddling is embarrassing to you and guaranteed to break the thread of what your interviewee might be thinking and saying. Remember, too, that tapes can be tampered with and do not make wholly reliable evidence of what was said if disputes arise.

Resist bringing all your armoury out at once and laying it on the table, an action guaranteed to frighten all but the most robust interviewee. Ask if he is happy with the use of a recorder (unless you have established this point when you arranged for the interview to take place) and produce your tools casually over the first few moments while you're talking in a friendly manner before the interview begins. He won't agree? Undoubtedly some people are inhibited by the realisation that a bit of electronic gadgetry is remorselessly docketing their every breath. If this happens you'll have to rely on your own writing; the weeks or months you spent learning shorthand will pay dividends and with practice the speed of your best scribble will increase. I can't overemphasise the value of learning shorthand even though it now seems such an old-fashioned skill. Modern devices have their uses (and you won't find a keener enthusiast for them than me), but they do not and cannot replace shorthand in every situation.

If you will be taking notes by hand, have your notebook comfortably on your lap rather than on a desk or table. You will be able to relax more easily and (more importantly) your eyes will have less distance to travel between your notes and your interviewee's face, so you will not need to be constantly dropping and lifting your head. Even keeping your subject in the corner of your eye while you write on your notepad can be revealing; the less jerkiness there is between question and answer, the more natural the conversation will be, and the smoother the interview. It is always sensible to check how long the interviewee expects the interview to last and that you didn't forget your watch. Put that on the table as well if you will be able to see it less obtrusively there, or keep it on your wrist if you can look at it without his noticing.

Make sure you can clearly see your interviewee and your notebook, especially if daylight has faded or will fade during the course of the interview. Resolve to speak clearly so he can hear you without any difficulty and, above all, to concentrate. When you are both settled and there has probably been some initial small talk (but not too much), it will be up to you to set the interview rolling. Don't let it roll for long before establishing your theme, i.e. what you're there for, what it is that's going to interest your readers about this man, and what he's going to say about it.

If you've never met your interviewee before, it can be difficult to keep your mind on the job at the beginning. It is quite natural to be a little nervous; some interviewers, like some actors, claim it keeps the adrenalin flowing for optimum performance. Once I interviewed a stage star whose handsome face I'd often seen in magazines, but a close encounter with this theatrical demi-god turned me weak at the knees. Could anybody be so devastating? He, long accustomed to interviews and swooning females, laughed and turned on more charm before I managed to clear my head and remember my assignment.

On the other hand, if you find yourself reacting adversely to an interviewee who adopts a superior or semi-hostile attitude when facing the press, it's important not to show antipathy. Shed any irritation you might have and try to remember that empathy is about showing you understand your interviewee's problems. You want to get something out of him, so a degree of rapport is necessary, even if it can't always be entirely genuine. Strangely, after a job well done there might be a certain amount of grudging respect in the air; you may even have softened his earlier opinion about you and the paper you stand for.

Always try to be relaxed in your attitude and remember you are conducting an interview, not an interrogation. It is best to be friendly (but not too familiar) and not to be so keen to frame your next question that you don't listen to what the interviewee is saying. Spot other points, too, that give you information without being put into words. As your attitude and tone of voice will affect the interview, particularly at the beginning, so will his. Listen to his body language as well as his words. Experts will tell you crossing the knees towards another person is a sign of acceptance or interest. Gestures with glasses or cigarettes and fidgeting with hair or jewellery are very revealing if you know how to interpret them.

If you cannot get an answer, or what you consider to be a satisfactory answer, to a particularly tricky question, don't resort to veiled threats. 'So I can tell readers you won't answer . . .' will only antagonise an already reluctant interviewee who feels himself temporarily forced into an unwelcoming corner. Most of all, avoid paraphrasing what he has said with 'So you are saying . . .'. The first (and only) time I tried this I was coldly told, 'No. You are saying that.'

Guard against subconsciously steering your questions in a direction that will ease the later writing of the interview if they do not naturally fall in such a pattern, and don't be frightened to acknowledge a mistake if you make one. If you find yourself inserting extra questions that didn't occur to you until you're face to face, fine. You're relaxing with a natural sincerity that will be welcomed and matched in spontaneous replies. For he may also have been nervous when you started.

The side of a large lake in a remote part of Staffordshire was the setting for an interview I've never forgotten. My interviewee was a woman of mature years who had established a remarkable friendship with a family of foxes living near the lake, which was within half a mile of her old farmhouse. After our greeting I realised she was trembling violently. Why? We were on her home ground, at her request. There was nobody else in sight and probably nobody for miles around. It was broad daylight and there was nothing for her to fear. It came as quite a shock to realise the only thing she could be frightened of was *me*. Since then I've always made an effort to look at a forthcoming interview through the interviewee's eyes, and very often this has helped both of us.

On another occasion, when an elderly man confessed he was petrified at being interviewed I reminded him that for more than four hours he had, single-handedly and in the teeth of a gale, held on to a young boy dangling over a crumbling cliff until emergency rescue services arrived and that without his incredible bravery the child would certainly have fallen to his death. This courageous man shrugged off his heroism but was visibly more at ease when I told him he was a VIP. 'Water on the Brain,' he laughed. I didn't understand his comment. 'Novelist Compton Mackenzie,' he explained. 'He was the first person to coin the term Very Important Person in his book in 1933.' You learn something every day.

With the interview going well, you'll understand why I say interviewing is so enjoyable. Let your subject do the talking and only guide the drift or intervene to ask questions. You'll find yourself seizing unexpected openings, earning unforeseen bonuses with, perhaps, a confession of your own ignorance or an extra depth of understanding, and all the time you're at the centre of a fascinating and often heart-warming conversation. Even though this is a deliberately set-up interview, being genuine is at the heart of all worthwhile communication.

One way into a verbal cul-de-sac is to get sidetracked too far from your intended course. At all times you must be in charge of the interview and the direction it is taking, with a light and apparently innocent touch, guiding but never forcing the interviewee towards the answers you hope he'll make. Push him and he may dry up on you. Be aggressive and he'll prickle. Being in charge does not mean being inflexible, for sticking doggedly to your plan could make you miss those informal gems he'll let slip when he's at ease. It will help to let him lead at the emotional level; at these times, often late in the interview, you can ask a 'risky' question almost as if you've only just thought of it – and that is when he might give you some of your most valuable information.

Sometimes a moving recollection or response is best greeted with nothing more than a nod or gentle smile, for there is a time to keep silent in most interviews. He could need a short break (and so could you) to recover himself and as long as it doesn't last too long this can be useful; while he organises a cup of tea, lights a cigarette or just blows his nose, you will be catching up on what's gone so far and what's coming next.

Enjoyable as it is (nearly always), you are there to do a job and nothing better can drop into your lap than a revelation. Your interviewee springs some big news: he got married yesterday, he's running for Parliament, he's left his wife of thirty years – or whatever, in his context, is news. Suddenly you have a news story as well. It can't be wasted in an interview that might not be printed before next week and you have all the research material about your man at your fingertips.

Part three – writing it

You take home a bundle of notes, a couple of full tapes and a headful of images; you can hear his voice, visualise his mannerisms, feel the friendliness (or otherwise) of his house and taste the almond on his wife's fruit cake. How is all this to be translated into a written interview? This is the third part of Gaul.

Back to reality and you recall your job is for a newspaper, which means catching the readers' attention immediately. Consulting your original draft for the interview may give you some of your structure, but after the interview you will be ready with a fresher, closer and brighter start; indeed you may decide to abandon all your first thoughts and intentions. The enthusiasm and spontaneity that rub off a charismatic interviewee are invaluable in carrying you through the writing-up of the interview, as long as you don't get carried away. You were there and your readers were not, so your task is to make them feel that it was they, not you, who heard your interviewee's voice, felt his friendliness and even tasted the fruit cake. And if 'he' was a gorgeous blonde, they want to 'see' that as well.

Did your interviewee say anything to make a good opening quote? 'I love getting married. It's being married I don't like' was my intro to an interview with a thrice-divorced actress personality currently dating a youngster half her age. This had been her answer to a question she had mused about without any prompting from me. 'I suppose you wonder who my next will be?' Her eyes undressed my paper's 45-year-old photographer and flickered away. His face was a better picture than any he'd ever taken. Another good opening might be something that made you laugh during the interview, recorded either directly or indirectly, or an aspect of the interviewee that particularly moved you and will move readers.

Despite the limitations of a narrative style, it has a few advantages worth borrowing in moderation; you can set the scene of the interview to help readers picture it, you may skip over less interesting periods of your interviewee's life or experience, and you can intersperse direct quotes with information about his background, where appropriate. You can also use flashbacks as long as they do not take over the main stream of the write-up.

How much of 'you' is there going to be and how are you going to present yourself? Are you to appear as a friend, a colleague or just a disembodied and even unidentified voice? And how are the questions to be posed – every one in direct quotes ('What do you most want in life?') or occasionally dropping into indirect speech ('I asked him what he most wanted in life?') to avoid monotony?

On the whole nothing makes an interview more alive on the published page than direct quotes; bearing the balance of the copy in mind, the more you can include the better and for these you'll bless your voice recorder. Writing all or part of the interview in the present tense may also keep it light with a friendly impact. Beware, however, of being too informal, lest readers feel you have treated your interviewee flippantly, especially if the theme, i.e. why you are interviewing him, is of a sensitive or serious nature.

Your deadline may determine how soon you write up your interview, but I advise doing it as soon as possible while it's still fresh in your head. This gets the job done, leaves you free for other work and lessens the danger of involuntarily imagining something was said when it wasn't. Did he mention such-and-such which you didn't write down, or has the thought supplanted the words because you hoped to hear them? There's nothing like words on paper for reassurance if you didn't use a recorder.

A sting in the tail?

Perhaps it is the unpredictability of interviewing that gives it that special satisfaction, but I can't pretend the surprises you might encounter are unfailingly welcome. Unwanted distractions can wreak havoc with your carefully planned half-hour. Your interviewee may fancy a couple of floppy spaniels on the sofa, a background of fortissimo Wagner and boisterously inexhaustible toddlers given free access to the interview. How tolerant should you be? A wife/mother/secretary may break in with messages, requests and general diversions. Do you smile gamely through them all for fear of upsetting your interviewee? That is another reason for fixing your interview location as tactfully as you can in the first place. A friendly greeting or pat on the head to interrupters on two or four legs is one thing; an interviewee constantly distracted and not properly listening to your questions or giving merely surface responses may mean a ruined interview.

Sometimes those seasoned in the business of being interviewed arrange the 'multi-interview'. You have assumed it will be a one-to-one affair, but no; you arrive to discover a 'minder' or two is to sit in the room with you, perhaps even answering for your interviewee or fending off questions he doesn't like. Usually in these circumstances you won't be the only interviewer either, so the event resembles a mini press conference more than an interview. If you do find this happening to you, without any fore-warning or contrary to what you have been led to believe would occur, it is generally best to cut your losses and leave. You won't be missing much, for any exclusivity will be lost. A press release about your potential interviewee will supply whatever your editor might want to see, if he's still interested; but a write-up from a press release is very different from the result of a live interview.

Where a child is involved as an interviewee, or in an important supporting role, it is expected that a parent or adult will be present. In these circumstances you will have to trust that the adult does not interfere or restrict the course of your questioning, and rely on your own reserves of gentleness with the child and patience with the adult.

A top newspaper interviewer told me that only once during more than forty years of interviewing had he been threatened about what he must or must not write. He demurred, the threat was repeated more sternly and my colleague walked out. No interview was published. As for bribes, 'No such luck!' laughed my friend. Both, of course, are to be treated with the one response the interviewee doesn't want – exit.

It sometimes happens that an interviewee lets slip an unguarded remark or comment that he almost immediately wishes to retract. He may apologise, be embarrassed and ask you to ignore what he said. One can only be guided by circumstances, but when a genuine mistake has been made it is sensible to agree to the retraction in most cases. To fall into the trap (as some media interviewers do) of pouncing on such slips with glee is poor technique and unlikely to benefit anyone. Your interviewee will be upset and/or annoyed and whatever co-operation you may have established will instantly be lost.

A request that you should keep a particular statement 'off the record' is not quite the same. I dislike being put in this position, for I am being asked to lay aside the interviewer's hat and – for a few moments, perhaps – be a personal friend. It's not that I don't want to be friendly (I usually do) but the interviewee is suddenly and unjustly assuming control of the interview. For decency's sake I am obliged to observe whatever confidentiality is to be kept, and do so, albeit the interviewee has taken advantage of me and my position.

Have you finished?

You've finished. The write-up is complete and you're ready to file it to the paper. Just a minute! Did you say anything to your interviewee about letting him see what you'd written before it goes for publication? Frankly, I hope you did not. It's a tricky point, and I well understand the comfort of knowing he's satisfied with your copy. That way, you might tell yourself, there will be no complaints, denials or misinterpretation about what he did or did not say or mean. Bits he wants deleted can be cut out, in other places you can amend your copy to accommodate his second – or third – thoughts, and anything he would like rephrased is easily altered. Above all, you'll be in the clear.

The accepted ethic in journalism is *not* to let your interviewee vet your copy except in purely factual matters, if necessary. It may be, for instance, that he doesn't have an exact statistic at his fingertips while you're talking to him and would like you to include it. Then, of course, it would be unreasonable to refuse him the chance of making a later addition.

This practice of not inviting an interviewee to revise your copy is not due to stubborn pride or any sense of superiority about what you've written; any journalist fancying his copy is sacrosanct wouldn't last twenty-four hours in this business. But newspapers are about people. Imagine the delays if all copy had to be checked, possibly in long-winded detail, by the people it concerned; I doubt tomorrow's paper would be printed before the middle of next week.

There's another reason: to let your copy be 'passed' by someone who is hardly the best judge of what he may have said about himself will be undermining your credibility. If we don't learn to take interviews or do any other newspaper jobs and then practise and polish our skills, we will be wishy-washy writers of no particular value to any newspaper. That doesn't mean our early interviewees must be sacrificed for our own career-interest, but the reverse. Knowing (or assuming) the interviewer is capable and confident of doing a good job will give greater confidence to an interviewee as well.

All the same, complaints occasionally arise after an interview is published. 'I've been misquoted!' 'We never mentioned it!' 'The interviewer made that up!' There is little to be done when this happens. No editor wants to be involved in disputes and it could boil down to taking your interviewee's word or yours. You have your notes or tapes to support you if necessary, but the editor is the arbiter and he should be your ultimate support. He knows you, your reliability and your standard of work. Yes, he knows you can also make mistakes; you are human, as is your interviewee. Unless matters reach a crisis (which seldom happens), nothing official will be done other than sending a polite reply to the interviewee regretting the receipt of his complaint; you may never even know there was one. But now it is clear why the majority of interviews are commissioned pieces.

From afar

Interviewing by phone and even by correspondence is often done, but in my opinion nothing beats going and seeing for yourself. The best interviews get *inside* interviewees, which leaves telephone interviews out in the cold. A conversation by correspondence may be a little closer to the real thing. Yet in both these circumstances the word 'interview' takes on a different meaning; one may be the only way you can get a direct quote, the other could be a legitimate avenue of research for a personal profile, and both are perfectly valid means of communication. But unless you are extremely talented and/or experienced, neither will capture the impact and immediacy that gives your published copy sparkle and makes your readers feel they, too, were talking to the famous.

One extra task remains to be done after the interview is published. Write a brief 'thank you' note to your interviewee and slip in a copy of the published interview in case he hasn't seen it. Then you're ready to move on to your next one.

6. Research and Help

Before you've had anything published in a newspaper (and especially if you are beginning to fear you never *will*), you may think established freelances have a secret recipe hidden from you. Only when you get to know a few more closely will you have an inkling of what goes on behind the scenes. Maybe you'll never discover how many books they had to consult to find a single piece of information; that an obscure statistic took three months to track down; where they came across a fascinating anecdote; or how they managed to interview a celebrity who had hitherto refused to speak to the press. You don't hear about their cuttings files painstakingly garnered over the years or their precious 'contacts' books of people who can tell them what they want to know or at least point them in the right direction to finding out. Oh yes, established freelances certainly have recipes, and because they have worked long and hard to make them *individually* valuable, they will guard them closely and keep them secret.

In the same way, much of the help you gather round you as your writing life progresses will also be personal and of use only to you. Your own book of contacts, for instance, is worth a great deal. It will carry names of people you've found who can and will provide you with valuable information, listed with where to find them and just what help they provide. I am no artist, but I know where to turn for essential artwork or pix in a hurry. Or I can be confident that if my contacts can't help me quickly, one of them will know someone else who can. Often one contact will lead you to another in this way, and so your contacts increase and the book becomes even more valuable. Parting journalists from their contacts books is like depriving babies of mothers' milk.

Cuttings files

Second only to a contacts book in a do-it-yourself system come your private files of cuttings. These grow to enormous size as you snip and collect bits of information you hear, read about or gather together (some of the ways this may be done are discussed below) and very soon your files will become your best friends, because nobody will have exactly the same files to refer to. I'm not saying you'll be at a disadvantage quoting facts other journalists quote (facts are facts after all) but if you can support your quotes from your own cuttings files your copy will stand out as at least original and at best unique. Building your own files is not difficult; many writers are compulsive collectors of snippets of information long before they've thought about what use they're likely to be. Every newspaper you read, every book or magazine that comes before you, everything anyone says that just might come in handy, you either snip it out, copy it in your notebook or jot it down on the back of your hand. Easy, isn't it? Yes, until . . .

Stuff it all into an old cardboard box and one day you'll have to sort through it and decide how much is useful and what may be discarded (my discard pile is always so small when I sort out cuttings that I generally decide not to throw anything away after all). I advise preparing departmentalised cuttings files and putting your cherished cuttings in the right place at the start. It doesn't matter how primitive your files are; old envelopes clearly labelled but held together with a rubber band or in a shoe box will serve the purpose. Better and easier to manage are concertina-type files with large identifiable pockets that can be renamed. As your cuttings files enlarge you'll realise you need to make subdivisions of some sections, so off you branch into more envelopes, shoe boxes or concertina files. However you do it, keeping to an ordered system is one thing you'll have cause to bless frequently in the future.

Tidiness is not the only reason for keeping your cuttings in order: every item should be dated and sourced before you put it away. Reminding yourself of your source on the cutting itself, i.e. where you found it, is important and can make the difference between a helpful and a doubtful cutting. Even more important is putting a date on it. Imagine you dug out a cutting giving population figures in Manitoba, say, before 'last year's census'. The cutting has no date, so when was the census? How accurate are the quoted figures now? You don't know and you daren't (if you are wise) risk using it. There's only one thing to do with such a cutting: tear it up. You might be tempted to use it and could land yourself in trouble because you relied on the unreliable. Furthermore, it has wasted your time and space, so a cutting without a date is worse than no cutting at all.

A last word about cuttings files: let them be your servants but not your masters. It's possible a cutting is incorrect. Whoever wrote it might have made a mistake, and by relying on it without question you could be perpetuating that mistake. So check it, unless it's quite impossible to do so. And if that happens you must make a decision about whether to use it or not. If you decide not to risk it, something else in the file will set you off on another trail if you want one. Frankly, I can't imagine any writer could be short of inspiration when looking through cuttings, for my problem is having far too many with not enough time to use them. Your cuttings files will ensure you never run out of ideas.

Research and reference

Suppose you are writing a 'help' article and want to use an incident where a toddler went missing in a crowded shopping precinct. Could you advise readers what to do in such circumstances? How can you find out where to turn for help, whom to call first and the best way in which you – either as an observer or distraught parent – can assist the police and other helpers in finding the child as quickly as possible? These and many other questions will need answers, accurate, up-to-date answers, before you can think about how to write your piece. All you need to know in this and at the start of almost every project lies in a single word: research. In the first instance, that usually means consulting reference books.

Editors report that inadequate research is one of the main reasons for rejection – and sometimes checking what you *thought* you knew is the first task, as I discovered from a little item in *Book News*. Like other readers, I assumed 'haggis' to be Scottish: not so, apparently. A recipe for it appears in an 18th-century Polish cookery book and it was known for hundreds of years in several other parts of Europe. So where did it originate – and when? I wouldn't credit it with a positive history without checking it to my satisfaction. Another haggis bites the dust.

There are several handbooks listing titles, addresses, phone numbers and other details about newspapers. Some are published annually, so cannot keep pace with month-to-month or even day-to-day changes, but (that restriction apart) they are thorough and reliable. You will find further information about them on page 39. The essence of credibility is getting the facts correct and it is important to keep your method of research up to date. The following are virtually indispensable:

- *Research for Writers* (A & C Black)
  The latest edition of this brilliant book by researcher Ann Hoffman is now a well-established tool of reference, offering a wealth of first-class guidance and information. It is no exaggeration to describe it as essential to every serious writer. Through its pages you will be led to research in every field, and merely reading *how* to pursue your particular trail will whet your appetite to begin.

- *Hollis* (Harlequin House)
  This is an expensive but unique reference book for researchers. The latest (28th) edition is as rich a source as ever of contacts for finding just about anything. Containing a huge amount of useful information it costs £77.50, including post and packing.

It is always worth consulting reference books published years ago as well as more recent arrivals on the scene. This being so, you may not easily find what you want. Here are just some I particularly recommend, old and new:

- *A Concise Dictionary of Confusables* (Hodder & Stoughton)
  Was the villain hanged on the gallows, or hung? Is proficiency the same as efficiency? Does supine mean prone? To settle these and any other confusions, this is the book to buy.

- *The Concise Oxford Dictionary of Quotations* ⎫ Three for
- *The Concise Oxford Dictionary of Proverbs* ⎬ every
- *The Concise Oxford Dictionary of English* ⎭ writer's
  Etymology desk

- *Teach Yourself Correct English* (Hodder & Stoughton)
  An excellent buy if you're hazy about how formal or informal newspaper writing should be. 'The ordinary user of English would do well,' advises author B. A. Pythian, 'to copy the better features of journalistic writing: crisp, clear English, directness of statement, and sentences of digestible length.'

- *Chambers Idioms*
  Another little gem. The use of idioms and figurative expressions in our richly expressive language will lift your copy, enlivening your style of writing. But this book is more than a list of idioms; knowing the origins of many adds to a writer's understanding and ability to use them. With this dictionary, English will be all plain sailing.

- *Chambers Dates*
  This book covers such a diversity of topics (politics, literature, sport, business, people, exploration – you name it and it's almost certainly here) that it's a fine prop for all seekers after general knowledge as well as a ready reference. With more than 6,000 important dates listed, there should be enough variety for us all.

- *Body Language* (Sheldon Press)
  Invaluable information for interviewers and a useful guide at any time to what people are feeling, which may not be the same as what they are saying. Interpret other people's thoughts by their gestures, learn how to tell if someone is lying, and much more. Written by Allan Pease, an international expert on communication without words.

Lastly in this section, I draw readers' attention to the large number of reference 'books' now available on compact discs. These shiny marvels transform the long and sometimes tedious business of searching for information and provide almost instant help at the touch of a couple of computer keys. Of all the CD-ROM encyclopaedias available today, none can match *Britannica CD,* the complete encyclopaedia on a single disc, in breadth of knowledge, quality of information and ease of use. It covers more than 65,000 subjects in articles ranging from concise explanations to comprehensive expositions; and from historical treatments of subjects to coverage of current events. There is quick access to word definitions from the 10th edition of *Merriam-Webster's Collegiate Dictionary,* and close on half a million references have been compiled, edited and hypertext-linked to text articles for easy navigation. As well as this there are more than 10,000 links to pictures and tables. A powerful 'search-and-retrieve engine' replaces the two printed volumes to scan the 44-*million*-word database, presenting an almost unbelievable wealth of information on your screen.

Other CDs particularly helpful to writers are the *Oxford Writer's Shelf*, published by the Oxford University Press, *The Chambers Dictionary* and *Collins Electronic English Dictionary & Thesaurus*.

And getting the words right . . .

Words are the tools of the writer's trade and it is important to have one or more top-class dictionaries to consult. If you haven't looked at a modern one recently you may be in for some surprises. Try these:

- *Oxford Writers' Dictionary*
  Described as the 'essential style guide', this paperback is for all those concerned with writing style and the printed word. Do you write council-house or council house, Romania or Rumania, is it gypsy or gipsy and should vice-versa be in italics, and with or without the hyphen? While your market will be your first style guide, this handbook not only provides the answers (in default of others) to such questions as these, but also deals with familiar and less familiar abbreviations, broader aspects of usage such as capitalisation and punctuation, foreign words and phrases, proper names of people and places and how *not* to spell commonly misspelled words. How did I ever manage without it?

- *The Concise Oxford Dictionary*
  The current edition is much larger than its predecessor, has more than 20,000 new entries and is as up to date in content and presentation as it is possible to be. It has been completely redesigned for greater ease of use, and the definitions have been rewritten in straightforward everyday English, with an absolute minimum of symbols and special conventions. It includes entries needed for copy about the lives we lead, such as cardphone, kissogram, global warming, viewdata and user-friendly (yes, it is, too). Among the particularly useful appendices is a succinct guide to punctuation and its usage.

- *The Chambers Dictionary*
  This is a dictionary for the space age yet retains the comforting reassurance of a well-loved friend. It's a treasure chest for word-lovers (sharny, poodle-faker, coolamon) and you'll find yourself looking them up for the sheer delight of doing so.

101

Besides new words are literary words from the Bible, Shakespeare, Dickens and major 20th-century writers. There are business and financial terms (golden parachute, Chinese wall, white knight and poison pill, for example), scientific and technical terms like E numbers, thunderhead and AIDS, and all entries have easily understood definitions and uncomplicated pronunciation guidance. There's more: if, for instance, you don't know the size of A4 paper (the size used in the UK for virtually all copy), you'll find the answer in one of the handy factual appendices.

A good thesaurus is also invaluable and I have a fondness for:

- *Chambers Thesaurus*
  Drawn from the *Chambers Dictionary* database, this paperback word-finder is the perfect memory-jogger; it helps the writer struggling to encapsulate his meaning in a forgotten *mot juste*, and is most valuable to journalists, writers and reporters. A good thesaurus like this has a special fascination; every use enhances your personal command of words and increases your general knowledge. But its greatest attraction lies in giving a list of possible words that have more (or less) of a particular ingredient, are more (or less) formal, are more (or less) euphonious; that, in short, have more (or less) of the precise flavour sought by the writer.

Philologist Godfrey Howard is well known for his lucid and easy-to-use books, the latest of which is:

- *The Macmillan Good English Handbook*
  Compiled as the first guide to the use of English specially written and designed for ease of use, this most practical aid is highly recommended. 'Just flip it open and find an immediate answer to any grammatical or other linguistic problem' invites the jacket flap – and for the most part I have found this a valid claim. Clearly laid out and blissfully free from abstruse grammatical terminology, it is often a shaft of light when you are beset with the problem of locating the best word to use in particular circumstances.

Other help

What do you do if you know a book exists but you can't find it? Luckily for researchers there are folk who specialise in solving this very difficulty. They advertise their services in writers' publications or sometimes in the national or regional press. I can't vouch for the practical results of asking for help from any particular one, but on the whole I have found anyone offering this service is unlikely to advertise without a sound network of established contacts as the searcher earns nothing if unsuccessful. Always supply as much information as you can when in search of any book: the title and author, and if possible the date of publication and the publisher.

Library services

Don't forget your local library as the first port of call for any research task. And wherever you are, always follow the researcher's basic code:

1 Know what you need or want
2 Ask the right person or someone who can find the right person
3 Be polite and persistent

Every public library uses the Dewey Decimal system to catalogue books and understanding how it works will save writers time wasted by looking in the wrong place. Any librarian will be pleased to explain it to you (it is easy to learn) when the place is not busy. Most borrowers and readers who use the reference departments make use of only a small part of what is available to them; more delving into what's on offer could be a welcome eye-opener. News writers may have little idea of what is available until they 'discover' the joys of their public library. Just set aside a few hours for getting to know the way round yours and it could be the most valuable time you've spent in all your research. The library you find most useful may well be the one in your own town but there are plenty of others available.

All major newspapers house their own libraries of press cuttings taken from their pages, as it is the task of several employees to snip every separate topic and file it away. Writers have cause to rejoice that they do so, for enquirers to newspaper libraries are (in my experience) generally treated efficiently and courteously. Some libraries insist that the enquirer is a member of staff, although a commissioned or contributing freelance may be given more consideration than a stranger. If the library staff do not know you, be sure to tell them you are commissioned to write an article for the paper or have been invited to submit one, if that is the case. For some papers a commissioning letter is required before you may make free enquiries; mentioning that the editor or features editor has suggested you contact the library will remove any doubts. Anyone with time-wasting, amateur or unreasonable requests will not be well received. Enquiries should be succinct, clearly stating the date or approximate date of the required cutting or cuttings and when you need the information.

Unfortunately what may still be a free or inexpensive service to those with good contacts is likely to cost unknown beginners hard cash. 'Shall I risk it?' you may ask yourself when faced with the choice of paying for reliable information or making an educated guess. Just remember, your reputation now *and in the future* might be the price you have to pay.

The British Library Newspaper Library (Colindale Avenue, London NW9 5HE *tel* 0171-412 7353 *fax* 0171-412 7379) is housed almost opposite Colindale Underground station, with some offshoots in other parts of London, and is the largest library of its kind in the world. Access is by ticket only, which must be obtained in advance. Researchers are normally expected to go to the library in person or to send someone on their behalf. Helpful assistants take a deal of trouble over genuine requests. Newspapers prior to 1801 and weeklies are housed here and you may consult the library's microfilm.

The Press Association (292 Vauxhall Bridge Road, London SW1V 1AA *tel* 0171-963 7000 *fax* 0171-963 7192) has three regional offices as well as its London base. The others are in Belfast (4th Floor, Queen's Buildings,10 Royal Avenue, Belfast BT1 1DB *tel* (01232) 245008 *fax* (01232) 439246), Glasgow (96 Warroch Street, Glasgow G3 8DB *tel* 0141-221 8521 *fax* 0141-221 0283) and Manchester (5th Floor, 33 Piccadilly, Manchester M1 1LQ *tel* 0161-228 7717 *fax* 0161-228 7331). The PA has a library holding more than 14 million news cuttings and a photo library housing over 5 million images. Founded in 1868, it is the national news agency of the UK and Republic of Ireland and is owned by regional newspaper publishers. Here you may find cuttings on every conceivable subject covered from every imaginable angle. There is also a collection of daily events listed for the past five years, 'who said what' quotes for the last year, and an outstanding selection of standard reference books.

With every cutting, no matter where you find it, check everything: the spelling of names and places and all its contents. Do the same (of course) wherever you go and whenever you collect material from, for instance, officials in police stations, hospitals, and other public places. This is particularly important in times of crisis or urgency when facts are so easily – and innocently – incorrectly reported.

The trade itself

People in the newspaper industry and publications about it are helpful to freelances. Here is a selection:

- *The Press Gazette* (formerly the *UK Press Gazette*) (Quantum House, 19 Scarbrook Road, Croydon, Surrey CR9 1QH *tel* 0181-565 4200 *fax* 0181-565 4395)
  The leading weekly paper for journalists, covering magazines, television and radio as well as newspapers.

- *Retail Newsagent* (11 Angel Gate, City Road, London EC1V 2PT *tel* 0171-837 3168 *fax* 0171-837 0821)
  Published weekly by the National Federation of Retail Newsagents since 1888, covering the full confectionery, tobacconist and newsagent (CTN) business.

- *Studies in Newspaper and Periodical History* (3 Henrietta Street, London WC2E 8LU *tel* 0171-240 0856 *fax* 0171-379 0609)
  This takes a scholarly look at press history and was formerly published as the *Journal of Newspaper and Periodical History*.

- *The Author* (The Society of Authors, 84 Drayton Gardens, London SW10 9SB *tel* 0171-373 6642 *fax* 0171-373 5768)
  A quarterly magazine sent free to full members and for a fee to non-members.

- National Union of Journalists (Acorn House, 314 Gray's Inn Road, London WC1X 8DP *tel* 0171-278 7916 *fax* 0171-837 8143)

This table illustrates the current membership of the largest union in the world for professional journalists:

NUJ members	UK	Ireland	total
Freelances	4,680	585	5,265
National papers	2,526	569	3,095
Provincial papers	3,691	344	4,035

Part of the NUJ Code of Conduct requires members to 'avoid the expression of comment and conjecture as established fact, and falsification by distortion, selection or misrepresentation', meaning that they should not pretend that matters of opinion are matters of fact. There is a London branch solely for freelances, while others are attached to branches in other areas of the country. Prospective members have to be proposed and seconded for membership by existing ones. Contact head office for information about your nearest branch meeting. Freelances in all ways receive the same treatment as staff employees on newspapers and magazines. The union publishes a freelance directory.

- The Chartered Institute of Journalists (2 Dock Offices, Surrey Quays, Lower Road, London SE16 2XU *tel* 0171-252 1187 *fax* 0171-232 2302)
  This organisation was founded in 1884 and has accumulated funds for the assistance of members with legal and other problems.

- The Society of Women Writers and Journalists (110 Whitehall Road, Chingford, London E4 6DW *tel* 0181-529 0886)
  A society of professional and amateur women writers in every field.

Other help can come from an army of public relations folk who are out there just waiting for your queries. PR officers or departments of industries, tourist boards, arts associations, volunteer support groups, political parties, environmental organisations – it sometimes seems the world is only too anxious to give you useful information, and it's all free. Contact the promotions or PR departments of associations and organisations relevant to your subject and you may find yourself inundated with material.

I think so-called junk mail was invented for my delight. Everything non-writers might toss in the waste-paper basket with nary a glance I pore over eagerly. Free useful information lands on my doormat daily by the see-through wrapperful, and long may it continue to do so. Do you read yours? I've never directly sought the junk mail that comes my way. I don't have to. But whenever I read 'Tick here if you'd like to be on our mailing list', I tick.

If you're desperate for help with research, typing, wordprocessing, photocopying and similar practical tasks you need only look in the pages of writers' publications, where researchers, typists, owners of word-processors and folk wanting to edit and improve your work advertise their services. Most are honest people offering to help you and make their livings or add to their incomes at the same time; others are only out to get your money, and care nothing about your eventual success. Like you, I have no way of judging, except by personal recommendation from friends and colleagues, which are which.

You are not alone . . .

Writing is a solitary business. When all the guides have been read, the ideas tossed about and the research completed, it remains a matter of sitting down on your own and *writing* – for days, weeks, months, even for years. Meeting others of like mind may be more than an opportunity to get away from the word-processor or typewriter; it may broaden your outlook and strengthen your resolve. Only you can decide what you want. You may find members of writers' organisations and conferences a spur or a bore; helpful or hopeless; not to be missed or to be avoided like rejection slips.

Writers' circles are the starting point for many freelances. Among their members you will find writers of all sorts but one thing you can count on: whatever type of writing they do, they will all know the regional or local paper, where budding newspaper writers often count their first successes. I've found every group I've ever visited immensely friendly, but only you can judge whether the one you attend is going to be of value to you or whether it is just a talking shop of mutual and meaningless self-congratulation. Most writers' circles number amateurs among their members (who can start as anything else?) but an increasing number include writers published in all genres with a high level of achievement. I know many established writers who claim they owe much of their success to the help and encouragement they received from writers' groups and the friends they made as members.

If you would like to join a writers' circle but don't know of one in your district, you may find what you want in a directory that lists over 600. Now in its eighth edition, the *Directory of Writers' Circles* costs £5 post free and is available from Oldacre, Horderns Park Road, Chapel-en-le-Frith, High Peak SK23 9SY *web* http://www.cix.co.uk/~oldacre/

There are many residential and non-residential schools and conferences where writers of all types gather to socialise and learn more of their craft. So numerous are they that I have space to mention only the largest, probably the oldest and certainly the best known. This is the Writers' Summer School held in rural Derbyshire for six days every August. Further details may be acquired from the Secretary, Brenda Courtie, The New Vicarage, Parsons Street, Woodford Halse, Daventry, Northamptonshire NN11 3RE *tel/fax* (01327) 261477.

Regional arts associations regularly host lectures and tours by established writers (watch your local or regional press for details), and courses for writers are often organised by WEAs and local authorities. The service organisation for all regional arts associations in England (Scotland and Wales have separate Arts Councils) is The Arts Council of England (14 Great Peter Street, London SW1P 3NQ *tel* 0171-333 0100 *fax* 0171-973 6590).

The electronic writer

Freelances, like other writers, use word-processors and many make wide use of other computer gadgetry to ease their working days. Britain is now officially the home computer capital of the world. The level of personal computer ownership here is twice as high, per head of population, as in the United States, and higher than anywhere else in Europe. There are more than 8 million personal computers (the vast majority of them IBM or compatible PCs) now in use, in about 40 per cent of households in this country. These figures are increasing at a great rate, and do not take into consideration the vast number of PCs in business, and many more in schools, colleges and universities.

Nearly 45 per cent of homes with schoolchildren own a personal computer, compared with 30 per cent in 1990. With these statistics comes the other side of the coin: almost one in three children, and twice as many boys as girls, never or hardly ever read a book out of school, yet they will happily absorb the same information from their computers. The following dialogue was overheard by a colleague outside the British Museum:

Father to child: 'Shall we go and look at the Rosetta Stone now?'
Bored child: 'Better look it up on *Encarta* when we get home.' (*Encarta* is a multimedia computer-based encyclo-

paedia that produces sounds and pictures as well as text when you consult it on screen.)

Even if you haven't yet taken the plunge – or are hesitating on the edge of it – you are still part of the world of electronics, like it or not; we all are. Every time we visit a library, a bank or even a small shop, computers will be put to work on our behalf – helping find particular books we've asked for, checking whether editors have paid the promised fees into our accounts or merely printing out a little till slip itemising our change.

As working tools they revolutionise a writer's life, especially in research. Investigating the methods of 'online' computer research in libraries can save days and even weeks of working time and put information at your fingertips, or, more precisely, on the screen in front of you. Enquire at your library to discover whether your local authority offers an online service; if so it may work 24 hours a day, for computers know no set hours. Should you be in doubt about how to use such a scheme, how it works or how much it will cost, ask a senior officer of the library service to give you details.

Get online yourself and you can have at your convenience far more than access to libraries. All that's needed to take this step into a new world of information is a personal computer, a modem (a small box that links you to the outside world via the telephone line: one may be built into your machine or attached to it) and the easy-to-follow software program that gets you started.

Until you use a radio you are unaware of the wealth of programmes, music and information available to you. Computer networks are much the same. You can't imagine what you're missing until you begin to 'log on' to the Internet, the global network of computers and their interconnections, which will let you skip across oceans and continents to find any information you want. Every day about a million people worldwide use the Internet – so what is there out there for you to dip into?

Just today in an online session I browsed through some databases (see below) for information needed for this book and had a quick look at the main news stories in the daily papers. Another day I might search for information about, say, the history of shipwrecks round the Scilly Isles, the authors of the top-selling crime novels or the lifestyle of the beaver. Tomorrow I shall probably look at the weather forecast (as I am going to be out for most of the day) and read some electronic mail from colleagues and friends in Australia, America and Italy, as well as in this country. We are discussing how to train kittens and the best way to refill inkjet printer cartridges. Most of these friends I have never met; in the world of telecommunications, computers and humans talk to each other. There are no barriers of sexism, ageism or racism because you can't see the people to whom you're talking. And to overcome the problem of not being able to see your correspondents' reactions to what you say, since you are not talking face to face, electronic talking adopts a system known as 'smileys', which are looked at sideways. Here are a few which you just type into your text:

:-) That's a little smiley face
:-(You're sad
:-< You're *really* sad
;-) You're winking at someone

The electronic community is generally willing to help others and when online you may gain access to information never available through press cuttings or libraries, however specialised they may be. Being able to search online databases from your own home can be costly if you let it be so. But the costs are reducing all the time as technology spreads, and the benefits are mind-boggling. Don't be deterred by the word 'database'. It is nothing but high-tech jargon for a huge filing cabinet into which somebody has put facts and figures which can be revealed to you via your home computer. All this is available without ever leaving your home, and at the time of writing the price of computer hardware and software is falling as the usefulness of services on offer to writers is increasing.

A new electronic toy came my way recently: it comprises a CD-based software program and a pair of headphones with microphone attached. This is IBM's VoiceType Simply Speaking for Windows 95, which allows you to speak into the microphone and watch the words come up on the screen in front of you. Magic? You need to be patient at first, spending an hour or two repeating simple words until the program is used to your voice; anyone with a pronounced accent might find this a more protracted process. Then one must speak in a clipped, unnatural voice, taking care to separate each word from the next, albeit only slightly. It seems strange at first but soon becomes easy – and with some practice I have become more enthusiastic. There are similar developments from other companies – and no doubt in time the technique will be perfected by everyone concerned.

When you've done all you can for your piece, and made use of every scrap of help you can find and written your copy, does the research show through? Is it apparent to readers that you've been raiding libraries, filling in facts from reference books and quoting from cuttings that may already have been seen by too many eyes? Always remember that research used well is invisible. Only you must know it was ever there.

7. Any Questions?

'How should I present my copy to a newspaper?'

Although nobody would pretend that the appearance of an on-spec manuscript can make the difference between acceptance and rejection, there is no doubt clean and clearly presented copy is more satisfactory for everybody who handles it. Even commissioned work is better received if it looks easy to read; a sub-editor will approach neat copy more happily and be less likely to chop it about in sheer irritation. It hardly needs saying that your print should be crisp and clear – so discard worn-out ribbons and replace faint ink cartridges.

It is temptingly easy with modern word-processors to spread yourself into a wide use of fancy typefaces but it is not wise to overdo it. Whatever styles the paper of your choice may prefer and however attractive the feature pages may be, it is best to stick to the plain non-proportional non-justified format for submitting text. Take care with underlining text: to underline tells the typesetter to put it in italics. And watch your punctuation. A second's carelessness can turn a man's laughter into manslaughter.

There are other pitfalls. The keys marked 'i', 'l' and '1' are poised on the keyboard to trap the unwary. Be sure you know whether to type an upper-case or lower-case 'eye' or 'ell' or the figure 'one'. George 111 was last spotted in the editorial column of the *Guardian*, who should know we have never had a King George the one-hundred-and-eleventh.

Neatness means double spacing on one side of A4 paper, allowing wide margins all round (4 cm and perhaps 4 or 4½ cm at the top of the first page) with pages numbered, preferably in the top right corner. The first page is generally not numbered. Type 'more' or 'mf' at the foot of pages other than the last, and finish your copy with the word 'end' and the wordage.

There is no rule about how the number of words should be displayed, and common sense will be your guide. It is usual to quote to the nearest ten if under 100 and in fifties from 100 upwards. So 87 would be 90, 164 would be 150 and 1,263 would be 1,250. Never add 'approx', as if you might be sued for miscounting. It is also sensible to add your name, address, phone number (and fax number and e-mail address, if applicable) on the last page below your copy and the wordage.

Start the first par at the left margin but indent the first line of subsequent ones three spaces and do not leave an extra line space between pars. There should be only one character space between the end of one sentence and the beginning of the next. If you use a word-processor, do not justify the lines at the right margin.

Give your copy a heading and if it is a long piece (approaching several hundred words or more) break it up on the page by inserting 'crossheads' (they're sometimes called 'shoulders') in the text at suitable intervals. This is particularly important if your work is unsolicited, for editors thrive on headlines and a rapid skim through crossheads gives them an instant notion of what your copy is all about. Neither the headline nor crossheads may be used as you set them, but they will help the copy look more appealing on the pages. There is no way you can know how they will be used on the printed page (for you do not know where your copy will appear, nor what may flank it on either side) but at the submission stage what you are aiming for is ease and speed of reading.

You'll also need a 'catchline', which is a word or phrase at the top of each page beside the page number. Its purpose is to identify where your page belongs should it be separated from its fellows, and the catchline can be anything you wish. Choose 'cream', for example, for each page in an article about catering, and your pages will be numbered 'cream 3', 'cream 4', and so on. Any catchline will suffice, but be original at Christmas when there could be confusion if other writers also choose 'Christmas'.

If you're used to submitting to magazines, you may be surprised to learn that on the whole newspapers do not like finding a 'frontispiece' or 'title page' (call it what you will) attached to the front of the copy with details of who you are, what you are writing about, and so on. They are more interested in getting to the point – and that (they hope) is to be found in the first par on page one. So I recommend putting whatever you have to say about an 'on-spec' article in a brief letter and then plunging straight into your copy. Like this:

Dear Mr Jones

As a lecturer in Hotel Management at Sally Lunn College I enclose a 1,000-word article on the local job opportunities for young people in the catering industry, with details of practical training courses here and in the rest of Europe.

An SAE is also enclosed.

Yours sincerely

Of course, that important but brief letter will begin by reminding an editor that he commissioned the enclosed copy (if that is the case) on a stated date.

That's all, except that any previous success you have had with the paper should be mentioned. Unless your telephone number is pre-printed on your headed notepaper do not make a point of providing it, for an implied hint that the editor will rush to phone you may be misconstrued. Particular mention of rights offered will brand you as a true amateur and may also be thought of as arrogance on your part. Cut off any spare paper on the letter sheet so the fact that your copy starts on the next sheet, without any more preamble, is immediately apparent.

For your own peace of mind you will want to keep a copy of your work. In pre-computer or word-processing times such a copy used to be known as a 'black', because it was made by placing a sheet of paper underneath the top one with a sheet of black carbon paper between the two. Nowadays computers can easily be set to print two copies of each sheet, so be sure you don't forget to keep one of them in your personal store. There's nothing like a duplicate in your hand for the comfort of seeing what you've submitted. I confess I rely on storage on a computer hard disk alone for short pieces, or for items I know will be published within a day or two. This can be dangerous, and I do not advise it unless you're prepared to risk losing your copy altogether.

Use a pseudonym? If you wish to do so, no paper will object – but make sure the accounts department knows about it so you have no problems with payment. Banks are reluctant to accept cheques not made out in your name without special arrangements being made.

The frequency of publication will determine when to send your copy. Your subject may also affect it, and you will need to allow extra time for the placing of Christmas and other seasonal work. An editor may be more kindly disposed towards you and the world in general on a Monday than on a jaded Friday, and a quick phone call to his secretary or the telephone switchboard (if there is one) will tell you when he's coming back from his holidays. Maybe your copy will be enthusiastically received if it's the first he sees on his desk that morning.

Finally, the packing and postage. For two or three A4 sheets it is enough to fold them over once and use a 23 x 16 cm envelope. For more A4 sheets a larger envelope that will take them without folding is preferable. Do not forget to enclose a self-addressed envelope of the same size, adequately stamped. I decided long ago that life is too short for second class stamps so I always send copy first class, even when it is in no great hurry. I know it costs a few pence more each time, but if you're in business, you're in business . . .

To allay worries that your copy didn't arrive you could enclose with it a stamped and addressed postcard for someone to return to you, although few newspaper offices will be bothered to do so. It is better to phone the editor's secretary a few days after posting to check that it did arrive. If she knows about it, *resist the temptation to ask any further questions.* Should you hesitate about asking whether they have your copy or not (lest the editor consider you a nuisance before he's even read your work), you could send your copy by registered post or Recorded Delivery.

If you are invited to send your copy on disk make sure it is in the approved format and that the disk is without fault or flaw. As for word-processor format, Microsoft Word or WordPerfect are almost certainly acceptable, as are several other popular formats. If in doubt, ask.

'What are online newspapers and are they good markets for freelances?'

Online newspapers are screen-based versions of their 'real paper' counterparts and are easily read on-screen when your computer is set up to access the Internet. Establishing connection is not a complicated procedure at all and is, quite literally, child's play for many already. The first on-screen page revealed to you when you access your choice of newspaper will contain headlines and columns of text and pictures, as does any traditional page. Imagine you see a box listing the contents of the paper on other pages. You want to read 'Overseas news', for example, in depth

– and as you point to it your mouse pointer changes into a little hand to indicate that a click on it will take you to another page. One click and you have done the electronic equivalent of following a written instruction like 'turn to page four' or 'continued on page six', and so on.

In the United Kingdom, papers from *The Times* to the *Sun* are online; worldwide, at the time of writing, there are some 2,000 different titles. Such online newspaper publication is particularly important because it is global, not merely national: 65 per cent of online titles are based in the US, 15 per cent in Europe and the rest originate in various other countries round the world. Half are published daily, 23 per cent weekly and the remainder follow more of a magazine format, publishing less frequently and not concentrating their energies on selling news (where speed of publication is essential).

The purpose of online publication is (of course) to make money, but establishing first-rate and attractive websites (to host the pages that appear on-screen) is very costly. Hiring a site is even more expensive, and the copy has to be bought for the hard-copy (paper) version of the newspaper anyway. The German *Bild Zeitung*, the biggest-selling paper in Europe with a daily circulation of 4.5 million, has the most popular website in Germany. Its emphasis on scandal, sex and big money-winning competitions reminds UK readers of our high-selling tabloids where hard news may be difficult to find.

The downside of the scope enjoyed by online newspaper publishing is that it is also a major handicap in regional development. Whichever way they read them, readers of local papers are most interested in their own areas and the activities of people in their localities. People at a distance, and certainly those in another country, are of little concern to them. But online publishing will not be denied. Local UK newspaper circulation has fallen over the last twenty years and publishers are keen to grasp future opportunities. Where there's a will (or strong commercial incentive), there's a way. When the Newspaper Society organised an in-depth investigation into the 'Digital Future', they foresaw a bright prospect for the role of the regional press as the Internet, television and newspapers work more closely together.

So who pays the bills? There are plenty of advertisements on the pages of online papers, and most of their revenue (as for their paper versions) comes from the companies and businesses who pay to have their wares or services displayed on the

Internet. As 'circulation' cannot be recorded in the same way as it is when a countable number of copies are sold, advertisers generally pay according to the popularity of their products. Each time an interested 'reader' logs on to a particular advertisement on the paper's web pages (instead of buying a paper to hold in his hands) a 'hit' is noted – and payment for advertisement space depends on the number of hits recorded.

When it comes to writing for online newspapers, the method of payment for writers is far less clear. Nobody owns or controls the Internet, and many newspaper proprietors have been ready to demand all rights in copy they may wish to reproduce on the 'net', paying little or nothing for its use. The prospects for freelances submitting copy are hard to identify and our instincts as writers concerned with the medium of the printed word may be that the changes are for the worse. Almost every online paper is waging war with contributors over rates of pay, lifting copy without payment to writers, and failing to negotiate deals for the fair and honest reward for material published on the Internet. All the same I believe an equitable method of payment will be established in time, and good writers who embrace the electronic medium will set new standards for the future, safeguarding the quality of material destined to reach the ever-growing audience of PC users.

With battles on the Internet front making headlines for the industry, one of the fiercest has been raging on the remote Shetland Islands. For 150 tranquil years the *Shetland Times* has kept the local population abreast of the local news. Then a former editor who was sacked from his chair (and subsequently won a substantial settlement for wrongful dismissal) set up a website on the Internet and began publishing *Shetland News*, Britain's first Internet-only daily paper, with 200+ pages covering local stories and items of interest. It also provides direct access to news agencies (from which the *Shetland Times* gets most of its news), to other papers, local authorities and sources of news and information. The *Shetland News* attracts enough advertising on its website page to finance itself and is not breaking any laws. Its pages are updated every day from a cottage on the island of Bressay whose population is just 350. Amid such idyllic peace the editor, who had earlier been Scottish correspondent for the London *Times,* also works as a boatman and wildlife guide to tourists for four months of the year – while his online newspaper attracts more than 4,000 readers around the world every day.

The world's first hand-held electronic newspaper has been developed by Electronic News Services, a joint venture between Mitsubishi and Tokyo's *Sankei* newspaper. It can deliver thousands of newspaper stories and will be easily updatable during the course of a day. Ideal for travellers in crowded trains, they say. The electronic age has hardly begun.

'Do editors really want my pictures?'

Thousands of pictures every day appear in newspapers all over the world and many of them have been taken by freelance photographers. Certainly it is possible to take your own pix (as they are commonly called in the newspaper world), process them yourself and submit them with your copy. But note the word 'photographers' rather than 'writers': to be a writer is one thing but to be a photographer of the required standard is not within the capabilities of every writer, freelance or not. Reaching the necessary level of expertise is not just a question of being 'good' with a camera, even with all the aids to easy picture-taking offered by modern equipment: the fact is that virtually all newspapers have their own staff photographers who can do a better job than 90 per cent of folk who are writers first and photographers second.

Happily that does not mean freelance writer/photographers have no chance to sell their own pix, for they have one great advantage over staff photographers: they can be in the right place at the right time, when staff photographers are nowhere around. Feature work is most likely to benefit from the individual pix that only a freelance present at the time can supply – but, again, such pix will only be acceptable if they are of high enough quality.

Just how you send your pix to the editor of your choice will depend, firstly, on their urgency. If, for example, you have some 'hot' pix of something in the news you would be wise to telephone the paper as soon as you can (not waiting to have the film developed) and explain what you have to offer. If the editor or picture editor is keen he will arrange to collect your pix or undeveloped film or ask you to get them to him immediately. When there is no such urgency it is best to submit prints, with transparencies (from 35mm upwards) rather than prints if you are working in colour. Leading papers now generally expect pix to be supplied to them electronically but are often helpful if you cannot get them over in this way. For all, the golden rule is to ask exactly what format is preferred by your market. Editorial requirements vary from one newspaper to another; there is nothing so sad as a set of marvellous pix ignored on a heap in the corner of an office just because they are not what was wanted.

It is not easy to sell pix to newspapers, and if you do so you will generally find papers with a separate picture staff are likely to treat freelances more sympathetically than are those where pix are dealt with by non-specialist (and often harrassed) journalists who have a great deal of other work to do as well. Specialist departments understand pix, photographers and their problems, but (due to cost-cutting) they are a declining number. A further result of keeping costs low is the increasing use of pictures from agencies and libraries which offer papers cheaper deals for regular supplies of pix in a huge variety.

If you feel your professional standards are not good enough or that your technique needs polishing, help is readily obtainable from the Bureau of Freelance Photographers (Focus House, 497 Green Lanes, London N13 4BP *tel* 0181-882 3315 *fax* 0181-886 5174).

There is nothing to stop you hiring pix from agencies and picture libraries for your own use, although you will soon discover it can be quite an expensive business. But if copy for a paper will plainly not sell without pix you could investigate such sources. The *Observer Photo Archive on CD-ROM* is a vast collection of more than 2,500 pictures of momentous events in Britain between 1949 and 1989, arranged in more than a dozen easy-to-search categories. Contact the *Observer Photo Archive* (119 Farringdon Road, London EC1R 3ER *tel* 0171-713 4423 *fax* 0171-837 1192).

The Media Guide (see page 39) lists hundreds of picture libraries and agencies but the standard reference book to picture sources is the *Picture Researcher's Handbook* by Hilary and Mary Evans, published by Pira International (Randalls Road, Leatherhead, Surrey KT22 7RU *tel* (01372) 802000 *fax* (01372) 802238). Also invaluable is the British Association of Picture Libraries and Agencies (BAPLA) (18 Vine Hill, London EC1R 5DX *tel* 0171-713 1780 *fax* 0171-713 1211), which publishes an annual directory of its 300+ members, many of them with specialist libraries holding pix not be found elsewhere.

It is important to be sure any pix you use or take yourself are worthy of use. It is easy to shock and dramatise events, particularly with pix accompanying stories in themselves tragic or disturbing. Think carefully, therefore, before you dispatch to an editor any pix that may and probably will distress readers with a visual reminder of their own plight. If your story concerns somebody losing a limb, for instance, too close a picture of the point of severance after operation will be distasteful in a newspaper; gory details help nobody. In all the years Franklin Delano Roosevelt, former US President, suffered from paraplegia there was not a single instance of any photograph appearing in any newspaper showing him manoeuvring or being manoeuvred from his wheelchair to a vehicle or other chair, or of him limping on crutches for a few painful steps – which was all his crippled legs would allow him to do. This control on the part of the press may have been for political rather than humanitarian reasons, but I doubt if such restraint would be observed today.

'Don't editors send out rejection slips any more?'

The staff on newspapers are busy people, and unacceptable unsolicited copy is often simply thrown away. But the more caring editors still do writers the courtesy of replying, particularly when they have been in earlier correspondence. One of the most gracious rejection slips came from the editor of a Chinese economics publication:

> We have read your manuscript with boundless delight. If we were to publish your paper, it would be impossible for us to publish any work of a lower standard ... and as it is unthinkable that, in the next 1,000 years, we shall see its equal, we are, to our regret, compelled to return your divine composition and beg you a thousand times to overlook our short sight and timidity.

'When were newspapers first published in Britain?'

The first London newspaper was published in 1621, and by our standards it was a scant publication. Early papers were printed irregularly and usually consisted of a single small page, rather like a newsletter, with no headlines, pictures or advertising. Most of the news came from overseas and was weeks or even months out of date. A few years later parliamentary clerks were employed to write reports of debates in papers then called 'diurnals', but not until the restoration of the monarchy after the Civil War was the press given freedom to publish in a wide range of topics, with a ban on criticising the government being the only restriction. The first daily paper published in England, in 1702, was the London *Daily Courant,* and other papers soon followed, with the *Daily Universal Register* appearing in 1785. This was the first British paper to employ foreign correspondents and is now (even after a self-imposed shutdown lasting almost a year in 1979) the oldest surviving daily paper. You've never heard of it? Soon after its launch the title was shortened to the *Register of the Times,* and then simply to *The Times.*

The *Daily Telegraph* was launched when the government tax on newspapers was abolished in 1855; circulations rose and prices fell. By then there were ten London daily papers. Most of them cost sixpence, *The Times* cost sevenpence so The *Daily Telegraph* cost twopence. Competition has always been the name of the newspaper game. By the 1880s paper was cheaper, improved printing machinery was available and advertising became fashionable, supplying newspaper publishers with a second source of income, and cover prices fell again. At the beginning of the 20th century Britons could buy their daily newspapers for just one halfpenny.

The first of the press barons, as they came to be known, was Alfred Harmsworth, later Lord Northcliffe. His empire at one time embraced the *Daily Mail* (which was selling half a million copies a day within three years of its launch in 1896), the *Daily Mirror* (published in 1903 as the first paper to target women directly and, in 1934, the first to appear in tabloid format), *The Times* and the *Observer.* Newspaper publishing was very much a family affair with Lord Rothermere, Northcliffe's brother, helping to dominate the scene, joined by other barons: Canadian Max Aitken (who became Lord Beaverbrook) and the Lords Kemsley and Camrose. All the barons happily used their papers to promote their political aims, irritating prime minister Stanley Baldwin to such a degree that he publicly reprimanded them in 1931 with the rebuke – originally written by his cousin Rudyard Kipling – that they were exercising 'power without responsibility: the prerogative of the harlot throughout the ages'.

But harder times lay ahead: the restrictions of the Second World War and economic factors saw a steep fall in newspaper circulation and many closures; in the United Kingdom the number of national newspapers halved. The loss of advertising revenue, the introduction of television advertising, higher costs in materials and equipment, and dramatic changes in working practices, dealt both national and regional newspapers hard blows.

In the past quarter century huge advances in technology have brought about a new industrial revolution. Gone are the vast clunking machines that laboriously set lines of type in lead, to be replaced by sophisticated computerised typesetting systems storing information and, at a touch, transforming words into lines of type. In the United Kingdom the introduction of new technology was accompanied by serious industrial trouble with the print unions.

Eddy Shah led the way into computer production with *Today* in the mid-1980s but the technology was hugely expensive and quite new to everyone on the paper; breakdowns were frequent and costly; deadlines were often late or missed altogether. Eventually the paper was lost to Rupert Murdoch's News UK empire for production at his new Wapping site. That in itself was a front page story for many weeks, with some of the ugliest scenes in recent years witnessed on television sets all over the world. Whatever it did to industrial relations in the newspaper world, it proved to be a major breakthrough in publishing history. Within two or three years every major newspaper in Britain had followed Murdoch out of Fleet Street, and all had adopted the new technology. In a modern newspaper office each journalist has a desktop terminal connected to the main computer. On-screen in front of him (or her) is the article being worked on; a copy editor may have the whole of the page. Journalists can import other articles and pix, information from libraries and source material from all over the world; a copy editor can move copy around on special page-layout terminals until it fits the page. One push of a button sends the finished page to be transformed into a printing plate.

In late 1985 the Press Association (see page 104) moved away and little was left to remind Fleet Street of the great press world it was for so long.

'I've been told to ring in with my copy but how is it done?'

Copy is usually taken over the phone or by fax when there is not enough time for it to be filed in the normal way, for instance the morning after an evening event when a report is wanted for a daily or evening paper. Ask beforehand if you're not sure what time to file (i.e. ring the paper with your copy) or which number to call. When the time comes, you will need to be prepared with either your complete piece ready to read out over the phone, or with notes you feel are adequate. On this latter point let me warn you, from long phone-filing experience, that reading a 'finished' piece from notes is not easy and there is absolutely no time on the phone for 'Oh, no, change that to . . .' or 'Er, that's wrong. I'll start the sentence again . . .' So (until you've had long practice, and only then if you're confident notes will suffice), write down what you want to say before you touch the telephone. You needn't type your copy or write it out neatly if nobody but you will ever see what you've written. A scribble (but a *legible* one) on any paper is all you need. Of course, if you are faxing your copy it will need to be as neatly presented as any other you submit by the so-called 'snail-mail'. I've spent years covering live stage shows and use the time driving home, usually late at night, to plan my overall piece. Getting the first sentence straight in my head sets me off to a good start when I get to a piece of paper, even if the rest is vague at that point.

For telephoned copy, whether it be a news story, a report on a meeting or a review, have it in front of you and dial the number you've been given to reach the copytaker. When you are connected remember the single most important rule: *start by making sure the copytaker has your name*, with your phone number if the paper doesn't already know it. This may seem mercenary, but many a good story taken over the phone finishes with a quick 'Thanks, 'bye' from the copytaker and nobody but the poor reporter knows (or wants to know) whose story it is. That vital point established, say 'I've got a report on a council meeting,' or 'Here is a theatre crit,' or whatever will give a quick idea of what's coming – and begin.

Read your piece clearly and in phrases, giving enough of each phrase for someone who has no idea what you're going to say next to understand it. I've always found copytakers uncannily acute and quick. They may say 'Yes' or grunt or just wait (you'll probably hear the keyboard-clicking pause) for your next phrase. You'll soon get into the right rhythm. Be careful to spell proper names, words offering ambiguity (unless their usage makes their spelling obvious) and anything else not plain from your text. There is no need to labour over punctuation (that's what sub-editors are for) except to refer to 'point' or 'full point' (house styles vary, even on the phone) at the end of sentences, 'new par' when you're starting a new paragraph, and to say 'quote' before direct speech and 'close quote' after it. Tell the copytaker when you've finished and say goodbye. Don't ask for a read-back or if there are any queries, for there could be half a dozen other people queuing up to file their copy as well, especially if it's first thing in the morning and everything has to be put to bed by half past nine.

Only when you read your copy in the paper a few hours later may you realise that a mistake could easily have been avoided if you had thought to spell out a word here or use a different phrase there. Writing copy to be filed by phone is itself special; do it often enough and you'll find yourself instinctively avoiding words that might be misunderstood – and that can only be good for us and our writing skills.

'Am I allowed to accept perks when I am out working for a newspaper, if I'm only a freelance?'

Get an assignment to report a flower show or the royal opening of a hospital wing and someone will have to provide you with a ticket for the event or you may not even be admitted. On an official job (where the organisers want the publicity a newspaper report will bring) it would, of course, be foolish to expect you to buy your own ticket, stand in a queue at the gate, and so on. You receive your free admission ticket and off you go. Usually there will be another ticket for a friend (any photographer from the paper will make his own arrangements) and this may be considered your first perk – a little treat for a friend who has to do nothing. You do the job, file your report to the paper, and that's that. Or is it?

It may be more complicated – delightful, you may think – when organisers shower you with other freebies during the course of the job and generally treat you so well you feel obliged to write only nice things about them and their event. How could you mention that most of the flowers had withered and visitors complained there was no tea, or that the hospital wing was dirty and the royal patron was seen by nobody but a handful of officials, disappointing the crowds who had waited for more than two hours in a muddy field? Wouldn't it be ungrateful to write nasty things when you and your friend have been given bouquets of flowers, plants for your own gardens, the offer of a greenhouse at cut price and all the cream cakes you could eat?

The answer is not to get in such a predicament. Entrance tickets are perks to accept without comment, of course, or you might not be there to do the job, and the extra ticket for a friend is also quite acceptable. So is a cup of tea, say, if the occasion is suitable, and even a sandwich or a bun shouldn't compromise your conscience. These are normal social pleasantries, after all. Beyond that, beware! A sensible perk is one thing, a privilege for being in the position of doing it is (probably) all right, but before accepting *anything* ask yourself if the giver sees it as a bribe, albeit such a word would not cross his lips. And when the answer could be 'yes' – decline.

As a theatre reviewer you may be given the best seats because the publicity manager wants you to see and hear the show properly: fine. As a book reviewer you will be given the books to keep when you've done the job: again, that's normal practice (the only paper I ever found that expected its reviewers to hand them back and *'in pristine condition'* – soon found itself short of reviewers). But once I was offered a blatant reward to write a glowing account of a newly published book. It wasn't even a well-written book and I was gratified to learn some months later that the publisher had gone out of business.

Perks are an acceptable part of the job in certain circumstances. If anyone piles them on to excess I become embarrassed, squirm to get away, and am reluctant to write a word. So perks can be self-defeating.

As for that phrase 'only a freelance' – please don't belittle yourself by such thinking. Freelances provide as essential a service for newspapers as do staff writers, and probably work harder. Down with this old notion that freelances are second-best!

'Is there any way of selling everything I write?'

There certainly is! You want to sell everything you write? To have interesting and varied work, meeting new people every week? Above all, to know everything is commissioned by an editor before you begin – and that a pre-negotiated fee will arrive every month? If this is still just a writer's dream, you haven't thought of writing advertising features.

In every regional daily or local weekly you will find a page or several pages devoted to them. Such pages will be clearly marked 'Advertising Feature' and will usually carry a central or top-half piece of text surrounded by display or boxed advertisements to fill the allotted space.

Both the text and the advertisements relate to whatever the theme of the advertisement may be. Perhaps a new restaurant – The Haven – is opening in the town, and the text of the advertising feature will give information about the incoming proprietors, their previous work, what their specialities will be, and how they have redesigned the old premises to attract local customers, among other relevant information. If the page is tabloid size (such features are found mainly in tabloid newspapers) there could be about 400–500 words of text, with a half-page spread taking as few as 300 or so.

The advertisements around or under the text are paid for individually by buyers of the space, as are ordinary advertisements, but for these special feature pages they relate specifically to the business, event, or whatever the topic referred to in the text. The new restaurant, for example, will be surrounded by advertisements such as 'Give yourself a break from driving home' for taxi services, or 'All painting and decorating done by Williams the Decorators' or 'Baxters for the freshest fruit and vegetables – always available at The Haven' and similar related advertisements. Some advertisements will be paid for by local businesses merely offering good wishes to the new restaurant and its proprietors.

The space taken by the text is paid for by all the advertisers featured round it. Why should they be willing to do this? Generally the advertising feature is established to run for many weeks, not necessarily always in the same title but (to avoid boring readers with the same type of feature) perhaps in other titles within the newspaper group. When this happens weekly a different space-buyer will be given centre stage. So it's a case of each helping the rest in return for a spot in the limelight while enjoying several other weeks of having their wares or services kept before the public eye in surrounding advertisements. This diversity of spotlight offers whoever is writing the text the variety and challenge of interviewing people in many different types of business and organisation.

Advertising features are organised long before publication by the papers' advertising staff. Representatives will visit prospective buyers of space, to explain how joining an advertising feature as one of a group would benefit their businesses. Once all the advertisers and pix are lined up the paper will need the writer – you? – to provide the advertising copy. This is where the job becomes fascinating. You never know how many interesting people you will find yourself interviewing: a woman running a lace-making business from her cottage, a garage explaining do-it-yourself car maintenance for retired folk, the organisers of a local bowling tournament, a couple opening a health club in an old church – the opportunities are endless.

When you've made a careful study of advertising features and are ready to try your hand, simply offer your services to the editor of your choice, being prepared to supply samples of your previous published work if asked to do so. Editors *prefer* to employ freelances for advertising features rather than tie down their own staff on non editorial work. When you meet the editor and he is satisfied you are the person for the job, you will need to settle the pattern of work, the fee you will receive and the expenses the paper will meet while you're on the job.

Further advantages are gained by writing advertising features. The essence of the work is turning out concise, totally relevant and fresh copy of a precise wordage to a defined deadline: all excellent discipline for any writer. Don't let people tell you this is not work for a proper journalist. If they do, ask if they get paid for every word they write. You will be.

'Should I send an invoice, and when may I expect to be paid?'

Always send an invoice for newspaper work, for if you don't it's most unlikely anyone will ever pay you. An invoice is a simple bill, made out on your headed paper for preference, stating the title you gave the copy (if it has not yet been published) or the heading they gave it (if it has), the date, and the sum owed to you. This reinforces the wisdom of getting all details sorted out before you write a word; if a fee hasn't been mentioned you may not know how much to invoice for. An entirely speculative submission may have been accepted and you genuinely don't know the fee, so you could make a guess and hope whatever figure you quote will be paid: this sometimes works but tends to fix rates for future sales to the same paper – and you may begin to wonder if you should have asked for more the first time!

As for when to send your invoice: the sooner the better. To many freelances that means even including it with the copy. I prefer to invoice a paper a few days after filing commissioned work and immediately after publication if work has not been commissioned. The former I pursue to the death, if necessary, as all commissioned work earns (or should earn) a 'kill' fee if it's not used. Published material that was not specifically ordered must also be paid for, of course.

The practice of newspapers not putting your invoice through the accounts system until a month after the piece has appeared is regrettably commonplace. All too often this means your item appears in print in, say, the first week of July but you don't get paid until the end of August, i.e. the beginning of September. Even then perhaps you'll still be waiting because – guess what? – half the accounts department is on holiday. Towards Christmas and the end of the year the situation is often worse. Some papers even process invoices quarterly, meaning *four months* might elapse between seeing your work in print and getting paid for it. If you are on a commission for a series or a regular column, make sure there is a firm agreement about when you will be paid before you begin work. And the one-off story that you still haven't been paid for? You may be told the paper is waiting for some artwork or other material to accompany your copy, or that a new story broke unexpectedly and for the time being yours has been held over. If you are owed a fee, keep pushing, politely but firmly (see also page 150).

'Should I write to an editor with my ideas?'

On the whole, query letters fall into two groups: those sent before submitting copy, and others chasing it (commissioned or not) after it's been posted.

It is sometimes possible to write for a newspaper in the same comparatively leisurely time scale as you might use when writing for a magazine, i.e. when a known future event lets you write what is referred to as 'magazine' copy. The millennium celebrations, for instance, are being discussed at every level as I write this; it has given freelances plenty of scope for associated copy in virtually all newspapers, where articles are being published on every conceivable aspect of the coming of the twenty-first century.

But for most newspaper work the pace is crisper; more topical (if not 'today') copy is required. There is simply not time to write to an editor asking whether he would like to see your piece. When speed is important it is better to query by telephone. Whichever way you decide to make contact, take enough time to prepare your proposal. After all, this initial query could earn you a large fee, so don't rush in ill-prepared. Be ready with what you want to say, in the same format as when writing the piece itself; state what it's going to be about without cautious preamble; then give the editor or his representative (the features editor, maybe) details of its proposed length and viewpoint, if one is appropriate, and outline why you think it will suit him just now. Don't get carried away and offer more than you can be sure of delivering. But don't be hesitant about your professional ability either; if you have little confidence in yourself, why should he, who may not even know you, have any at all?

Now for the 'chasing' letter. Imagine you've submitted copy to a paper 'cold', without any previous contact about it, and you didn't take any steps to find out whether it was received. Weeks and months go past and you've heard nothing. Should you query the paper about it now? Of course if the intended recipient reports not having received it, any proof of postage you obtained at the time will be no help and its non-arrival will concern only you and the Post Office.

If you decide to query, it is better to do so by letter rather than by phone. Write to the editor's secretary (on a national or large regional paper) or to the editor himself, clearly stating the circumstances and enclosing a stamped self-addressed envelope for a reply.

More time goes past and nothing happens? Then phone the same office and explain your difficulty, mentioning your earlier letter. If, despite all this, the paper is uncertain about whether your copy was or was not received, you could assume they don't really want work from freelances. Luckily there are plenty of others who do – if you're in time.

'Shall I call on the editor of my local paper?'

Without any prior contact – NO! Editors are busy folk and sometimes those on the smallest papers are the busiest, having to do many jobs themselves.

If he has said he'd like to see you, ring the paper and ask when would be a suitable day and time, and don't be late. Never suggest meeting anywhere other than in his office. Whether the meeting is his idea or yours, take it as an indication that he is interested in your work and sees, or hopes to see, you as a useful contributor to his pages in future.

Be prepared with tear sheets of your work, especially newspaper work. It is wisest to let them speak for you, although he may not give them more than a cursory glance, but of course you could refer to whatever previous newspaper experience you have had if it is relevant to do so. Give some thought to what you want to offer him as occasional or regular contributions, and (if appropriate) produce some written ideas. Leave them with him if he's interested, rather than expect him to study them on the spot.

Talking to an editor face to face can bring practical benefits, so don't be shy. In discussing what you're going to write for him, he's bound to reveal his own likes and dislikes and his personal view of the topic in question. When he actually sees it in print a few days later, he will recall the conversation and (assuming you've followed his lead) is likely to look more favourably on your copy.

If you don't know the current rates of pay, ask. No editor will think any the worse of you for doing so; in fact most will instantly class you in the 'professional' category at such a question. When the reply is, 'Our usual rates,' it is easy to tell the truth: 'I could be out of date, so please tell me what they are.' Embarrassment when talking about money is as much an invitation to be paid less than your due as is demanding it before you've demonstrated your ability to file good copy. In the first case you could be taken for a ride, in the second suspected of thinking the fee more important than the work, which is a mistaken priority.

Don't get so interested in what an editor's saying that you forget the time. He can probably only spare you a few minutes; if you keep him from his own work for too long he might recall you as a potential time-waster rather than a valuable contributor.

'How do I know whether my accepted work was ever published?'

Assuming you don't see the paper regularly you could (a) ask friends who read the paper to look out for your copy, (b) persuade someone working for the paper to do the same, (c) ask the editor's secretary to send you the relevant copy(ies), (d) contact the cuttings library, if there is one, or (e) ask the editor to tell you exactly when your copy will be published.

Course (a) is probably the best if you have reliable friends who see every issue of the paper. You might opt for (e), which sounds trouble-free, but in my experience few editors want to bother with copy once it's gone. Both (b) and (c) could be wild shots if you don't know anyone on the paper, which leaves (d), the cuttings library, as the most hopeful course.

Regional provincial and national papers will provide you with a photocopy of your work on request, but what if the paper doesn't run to a cuttings library? You may resort to one of the cuttings services mentioned in Chapter 6, for which you will have to pay, of course. If everything else fails, luck may solve the problem. Once, when I'd missed an edition of a paper carrying some copy I particularly wanted to keep, I opened a well-packed parcel sent through the post – and there among its protective wrapping was my copy. I can't recall what was in the parcel, but I certainly welcomed its packing!

8. Business

I believe knowing (or hoping) we are going to make money out of what we write makes us take a more objective view of our work; it is a reason for writing – and supplies the detachment that is so valuable in marketing and editing what we write. Adopting a businesslike attitude does not sully the art of writing, as some folk claim. The truth is that if you mean business you have to be both a writer and a record-keeper. Because I want to be a writer more than I want to be a record-keeper I long ago devised a system that (a) demands little time, (b) keeps my affairs in order, and (c) satisfies the Inland Revenue. That is why I urge you to study this chapter closely; not necessarily to model your own system on mine, but to appreciate the value of getting the 'business' straight from the beginning. You won't regret it. Organisation and a positive attitude are necessary for success.

Status

It is important to resolve when you start writing whether you only wish to be a casual writer who indulges in the activity for a hobby or whether you are, or are soon going to be, a professional writer. Don't misunderstand that word 'professional', which refers largely to an attitude of mind; you can be just as professional when you only write a couple of articles a year as when you are filing copy every day to a top national newspaper. Nor is it in any way a slur on being a dabbler. Many writers want no other status and would certainly not wish to be caught up in what they see as a deal of paperwork and business hassle, especially if they have just retired from a lifetime of it. It is the quality of the finished product – the written word – that counts.

I'm always embarrassed by any suggestion that a writer is someone 'precious' (especially if the suggestion is made by another writer), but having a purposeful self-image is not arrogant. Being businesslike is itself good business. Working with your affairs and papers in a muddle will make life harder because you may not be able to find essential letters, agreements, disks and other references when you want them. Such confusion may generate mistakes and missed opportunities; it will also give other people the impression that you are not likely to do a good job of work with your writing when you're in a state of constant chaos. Getting straight in your mind as well as on your desk is not just a matter of personal satisfaction but one of practical importance. If you are a truly professional freelance writer you will find yourself more confident and able to deal with many working situations more capably.

Paying your tax

In April 1997 the task of self-assessment was imposed on all writers (and other folk) classed as self-employed. In general terms, this involves the taxpayer calculating the tax payable on income, rather than leaving it to the Inland Revenue.

When you earn money for your work, be it ever so little, the Inland Revenue will want to know. It's a mistake to think, 'A few pounds for fillers and some small cheques for articles I sold to X newspaper – that isn't worth bothering about.' Oh yes it is. Not only because there might be some awkward questions from the tax inspector when you become better known but because of those expenses you can set against any tax you might have to pay on your earnings.

Postage, stationery, telephone calls, printing headed paper and business cards, insurance (if taken out specially) and maintenance of equipment such as your typewriter or word-processor, tapes, disks, books of reference (including this one), travelling expenses, hotels, meals eaten out in the course of work, secretarial expenses, professional subscriptions; once you start noting your expenses you'll be amazed how they add up. You may also amortise the original cost of whatever equipment you need, a typewriter, word-processor, voice recorder or any other major purchase, by claiming 20 per cent or perhaps 25 per cent (usually subject to the capital cost and by negotiation with the tax inspector) of the price paid in the first year, another 20–25 per cent of the rest the following year, and so on, until the whole sum has been defrayed. Keeping your capital expenses in proportion to your anticipated income is only sensible, particularly at the beginning.

All income is now collected in one tax return and the tax is payable in one lump, although it may be divided into two parts. From past knowledge of our tax affairs the Inland Revenue sends (or should send) each of us only the appropriate pages to complete, but it remains our responsibility to see we receive them. All income from writing must be declared, as must income from all other sources. We have to declare everything on the tax return but do not have to send accounts. Of course there are many specialist firms (and a few sharks) who will do the work for you if you can't or don't fancy doing it. Banks also offer the same service for a fixed fee; 'tax shops' will need to know full details of your affairs and may charge anything from about £50 to over £200, competing with accountants for the work. If you decide to patronise a tax shop, check it carries professional indemnity insurance covering incorrect advice or negligence. Remember that *you* will be held entirely responsible for errors and mistakes, no matter who actually completed the forms or who advised you in doing so. Probably the wisest course of action, if you are not planning on doing it yourself, is to seek help from a qualified accountant, preferably a member of the Chartered Institute of Taxation or the Association of Tax Technicians. Whatever you decide, invest in a good tax guide. There is none better for writers than the annual *Lloyds Bank Tax Guide* by Sara Williams and John Willman (Penguin Books).

To gain the maximum tax advantage, be sure to keep your financial affairs in good order. The more you know about what you should pay under the new self-assessment, the less likely you are to be one of the many taxpayers paying an average of £304 too much every year.

If you are doing it yourself, complete the documents with a declaration of your profit and claim the allowances to which you are entitled. Send the return to the tax inspector before the end of the following January (the end of September in the year of assessment is the deadline if you are asking the Inland Revenue to make your calculations for you) and you will receive an assessment saying how much you have to pay. If you are late making your two interim payments you will be charged interest. If the final payment (due on 31 January following the tax year covered by the return, which is also the last date for submitting it) is not made by 28 February you will be charged interest and a 5 per cent surcharge, plus a further 5 per cent if payment is not made by 31 August. You have been warned!

In theory the government wants to cut costs by making tax-payers do the work themselves. In practice the self-assessment forms are complicated enough to send most people scurrying to someone for help. The final straw: don't forget to put a stamp on your tax returns before you post them.

Practical details

'The work had been more compleat, had I not been as much, during its writing, oppressed with taxes and almost weekly assessments.' So wrote William Lily (1468–1522), first high-master of St Paul's School, London, in *Prophetical Merlin*. Comforted by the thought that the time taken in dealing with tax dues is no novelty to writers and wanting to gain full control of your affairs, you might wish to work out your hourly rate of pay after, say, the first six months of working as a freelance. This can be a humbling experience, for by this I mean your hourly rate of pay on the whole job. My records of what I have achieved at the end of each working day remind me of the time I have given to research, to writing, to keeping records and to general pottering. Weighing this against what I shall eventually be paid for the work in hand, I can decide whether I should spend my time more profitably or whether I wish to indulge myself with a specific project in future, knowing it will not be one that pays for itself, let alone makes a profit.

Keep all the receipts, invitations, details of meetings, travel tickets and even diaries that come your way to produce for the taxman if he wants to see them; it's unlikely that he will, but he might. Everything that serves to demonstrate your status as an established freelance is worth saving. Are you attending a writers' conference or school to further your knowledge and experience? Claim those fees, of course – and the cost of getting there and back.

It may be hard to work out exactly how much your car costs you when you are wearing your freelance writer's hat unless you reserve the car solely for that purpose, which is hardly likely to be the case. Mileage allowances vary greatly, but you may be able to discover the rates your target market will pay and reach agreement that such expenses will be refunded. A written confirmation of the rate customarily granted to journalists on the staff of any paper you write for regularly may encourage the taxman to allow you the same rate. Otherwise you should put in a claim at a 'reasonable' rate – see the NUJ and Society of Authors' most recently published guides. It may be even harder to convince the Inland Revenue when you come to claim for car maintenance and depreciation as these vary even more, depending on the model, age and mileage of your car.

Do you work in a room in your house specially set aside for the purpose? You may legitimately claim for the light, heating and cleaning of your work room, plus whatever proportion of rent (if any) it represents in relation to what you pay. You should also be aware that although exemption from Capital Gains Tax applies to your house (or your main house if you own more than one), it does not apply to whatever part of it you use for carrying on a business. This means that if and when you sell the house you will have to pay Capital Gains Tax on the 'business' portion of it, assessed in proportion to the whole house. This penalty only applies to exclusive use of a room (or rooms) for your work, and tax is payable at your highest income rate. It is quite legitimate to claim that the room where you write is not exclusively a work room if you use it for domestic purposes as well, even if only occasionally. Anyone is free to work from home, but you may need planning permission if you want to build a special extension as a workplace. If you have a mortgage you should tell your lender what you plan to do; if your home is rented check with your landlord first; and if you live in council premises let the housing officer know.

On the brighter side, you will be able to claim expenses incurred before you actually earn anything at all, providing you tell the Inland Revenue from the beginning that you are in business as a writer. Your work may, for instance, take three or four years to research before a word of the finished product is written, and you may carry forward a sum covering 'work in progress'.

Because of the wide variations in tax law concerning employed and self-employed writers, it will certainly help to behave at all times as the self-employed writer you are. Use private headed stationery and work on your own equipment. Make sure you are paid on the basis of work done, not hours worked. Make your own arrangements for insurance, pensions and so on, and (probably the best safeguard against taxation at source) do not work exclusively for one market. It is hard to convince the Inland Revenue of your freelance status unless you work, or have worked, for at least three or four different employers in the course of a single tax year.

Some NUJ freelances move from office to office, working alongside staffers but getting no staff benefits, holidays, sick pay, maternity or parental leave, service increments, employer-paid training or even normal expenses. The advantages of their freelance tax status makes the work worthwhile, even with such disadvantages. Incidentally, be wary about accepting staff privileges when you do a small regular task, as this may affect your freelance status.

Writers with incomes from writing currently greater than £47,000 per year must, like everyone else in the same boat, register as payers of Value Added Tax with HM Customs & Excise. Those earning less than this figure may also register, at the discretion of HM Customs & Excise, and may obtain certain benefits thereby.

You may feel the beginning of your writing career is littered with traps and perils for the innocent; you have no desire to defraud the Inland Revenue and are frightened of unwittingly doing so. Take heart. If your bank manager or friendly solicitor is helpful but lacks the particular expertise required in this field, a whole army of tax advisors has leapt to help fill in self-assessment forms – for a fee. The Citizens' Advice Bureau may also help; although its staff may not be quite specialised enough for your circumstances, they and other community enterprises offer free advice and will at least tell you where to find more.

Good record-keeping is wise. With it you needn't fear the shadow of the Inland Revenue, while also being fair to your own pocket.

Your records

With your professional status you will be either a full-time freelance with a steady stream of work accepted and paid for during the year, a 'hobby' scribbler with a different full-time job, turning winter evenings into success in a handful of publications, or somewhere in the varieties of writing that lie between the two. Whichever category of freelance writing you fall into, taking trouble with record-keeping now, as you go along, will save you a great deal more trouble later.

The best method is simple to use and understand. In all aspects of writing it's a mistake to let the tail wag the dog by setting up a method you can't instantly recall when you pick it up after being away. A hard-backed book with lined pages is ideal as an 'expenses book'. Rule a few columns as you wish, and make it a habit to log whatever you spend every day, as well as every mile you travel, every phone call you make and every stamp you lick. (Actually this last can be a chore; I buy sheets of stamps to be used solely for business mail and keep them in a special pigeon-hole in my desk, so they don't get confused with other stamps used for domestic and private letters.) I've always found it easiest to record my entries only on the right-hand pages of an expenses book; the book naturally falls open with the right-hand page facing me waiting to be written on and, such is the usage it gets, it usually presents itself to me on the current page. I paper-clip receipts relevant to each page on to the left-hand pages.

Just as simple is a system of keeping track of manuscripts: where I send them, when, and what their fate is. All details are kept in a database on the hard drive of my computer, but for safety's sake I record them on paper as well in what the computer world calls 'hard copy'. Each piece of work I do, be it long or short, is given a number in my manuscript book. This number, incidentally, also identifies the work when in due course it is pasted in one of my archive albums. I acquire the large hard-covered albums used by commercial printers to show their potential customers Christmas cards and other lines. If you would like to do the same, find such a printer and ask if he will give you several of these albums when he's finished with them (which will generally be in the early part of the year). Most printers will readily agree, especially if you have tactfully used their services yourself, as they only throw the albums away when their display of current cards is out of date. I have dozens of such albums for my archives and find they serve the purpose ideally. They are easy to label, printed tear sheets show up well on their pages, and their sturdiness retards newsprint from yellowing with age.

My manuscript book also records the title and length of each item of copy, with the date on which it is dispatched and its destination. Then follows a space awaiting news of its date of publication and the fee paid, also with its date. I know a commissioned piece of work will be sold without any fuss (or I've gone horribly wrong somewhere), so only a few blank lines will be needed to record its history. I can leave a little space for forthcoming details, rule a line across the page and start recording the next piece of work below it. Only when I am not sure how long it might be before a piece is accepted, published and paid for will I leave plenty of space for its history. I don't like copy with a long history. To the left-hand page opposite the work I paper-clip correspondence, agreements, payment letters and any other relevant pieces of paper. Pages at the back of the book also record which papers have bought my copy, when and their rates at the time. At the same time I keep on disk an instantly accessible spreadsheet showing me full details of all the above at the touch of a key. Like many writers, I'm in love with my word-processor and cannot now imagine writing anything without it; the ease with which the computer also deals with accounts, keeps records and presents me with instant assistance in all aspects of the business side of a writer's life is like a trusty friend taking some of my workload off my shoulders.

Because writers without any other job or profession are self-employed and 'on their own', you might need to think of taking out a private pension, planning your tax distribution over the years, or making personal insurance provision. You'll soon find that dealing with all this is a considerable intrusion on your writing time; in these matters, and in others, an accountant with specialised knowledge and experience in this field will be invaluable – and you can, of course, set his charges against tax.

Being a professional

Many folk are surprised to know there are no compulsory qualifications for writing for newspapers: what happens is that most editors hire on the quality of your last deadline or the most recent work portfolio you can show them.

To assess the current training position, we need to differentiate between making journalism a full-time career and using it as a part-time or occasional source of income. Recognised schools and colleges cannot take all the young hopefuls keen to enrol as trainee journalists, so let's deal with the career side of it first.

To make it a lifetime's work, it is wise to start early – while at school or college. Lord Northcliffe said, 'The only way to teach people to write is to have them write.' But training is not a substitute for education, and what are called 'media studies' are threatening to push aside real journalistic values and skills in some teaching colleges. Running the local students' paper, the rock band's weekly news-sheet or regular support letters for the football team may seem far from what you will later be thinking of as 'journalism', but all such occupations present young writers with a chance to see if they have (or can acquire) the essential tool that will serve them all their working lives – the ability to write: to say what they mean to say clearly, putting the right words on paper in the right order, at the right time and in the right way for the people who are going to read them.

The Newspaper Society (74 Great Russell Street, London WC1B 3DA *tel* 0171-636 7014 *fax* 0171-631 5199) takes a broad interest in newspaper training and promotes NiE, the Newspapers in Education scheme which oversees some 66 educational projects linking schools and newspaper companies. A booklet titled *Making the Decision* from the Newspaper Society lists accredited courses.

For a full-time career a first degree is virtually essential. Your path may then take you to a local paper, where four out of five trainees now start. Because journalism is fashionable you will not earn much at this stage, maybe finding this a disappointment after earlier high hopes that the world would fall at your feet once you put your foot on the ladder; at the time of writing, a starting salary of less than £10,000 a year is commonplace. Outspoken writer Vera Brittain (1893–1970) had strong views about young graduates too full of their own importance. 'The idea,' she wrote, 'that it is necessary to go to university in order to become a successful writer or even a man or woman of letters (which is by no means the same thing) is one of those fantasies that surround authorship.' Of course she was quite right. A few local papers will still accept non-graduates and if you find yourself a place on one and do not have graduate status you will certainly need at least three A levels in suitable subjects: English, history and economics, for example.

Poverty and low pay are endemic in training but at least the situation in this country is not as bad as it is in the United States. There, crazy agricultural protectionism means that each American cow gets more subsidy than an American university student. In the UK many young trainees in journalism feel they are lucky to be paid £6,000 a year when others on work experience are paid nothing at all and just get a little for expenses or fares. It is common for papers to pay less now than they were paying ten years ago. The NUJ is arguing for a minimum salary of £15,000 for a newly qualified journalist and £20,000 for one with two years' experience – less than the average non-manual wage. The position is currently worse for women than for men, for coloured people of both sexes, and for writers in rural areas.

At the same time the *Sunday Times* reports that, of Britain's 500 wealthiest people, brothers David and Frederick Barclay, owners of *The European*, *The Scotsman* and *Scotland on Sunday*, are worth £500 million, Conrad Black, proprietor of the *Daily Telegraph, Sunday Telegraph* and some 60 Canadian daily papers, weighs in at £250 million, Mohamed al Fayed (*Punch* and the *Liberty* radio station) £1,000 million and Viscount Rothermere of the Daily Mail and General Trust £1,200 million.

In truth you may not be of much value to the paper employing you when you start: you need proper training in the craft of journalism itself. More than half the companies running local paper groups have their own training departments (as do many magazine companies) and, whatever your degree status or scholastic achievements and whichever way you approach your career, an approved apprenticeship must be served. To make the very best of it you will, at the least, have an abiding curiosity, an awareness of logic and order, and a love of words. Without these, university degree or not, you are a non-starter.

On a local paper you will learn what may appear to be small skills that will nevertheless be invaluable to your future career: how to write funeral reports, keep lists of wedding guests, submit inquest verdicts, take notes on proceedings at council meetings, interpret court reports accurately, and many other apparently mundane daily tasks, all to precise deadlines. Working to a deadline is more than a challenge: it is positively beneficial. Without a deadline by which material is to be completed, work tends to drift between stages of rewriting, scrapping, beginning and rewriting in a permanent state of metamorphosis in which nothing worthwhile is completed.

Some newspaper groups run their own training schemes and recognise their own qualifications for reporters. Among them are:

- The Editorial Centre (formerly the Westminster Press Training Centre) (Hanover House, Marine Court, St Leonards on Sea, East Sussex TN38 0DX *tel* (01424) 435991 *fax* (01424) 445547)
- Johnston Training Company (Upper Mounts, Northampton NN1 3HR *tel* (01604) 231528 *fax* (01604) 250186)
- United Provincial Newspapers (Wellington Street, Leeds, West Yorks LS1 1RF *tel* (0113) 243 2701 *fax* (0113) 244 3430)

However a start is made, journalism training is invaluable. Young trainees are taught many vital skills in what is either a day-release programme (taking time from their normal work on the paper) or a year's pre-entry course. Available to them are a large number of options, ranging from Higher National Diploma to degree and postgraduate courses accredited by the National Council for the Training of Journalists (Latton Bush Centre, Southern Way, Harlow, Essex CM18 7BL *tel* (01279) 430009 *fax* (01279) 438008) and the Periodical Training Council. The NCTJ is a charity running a wide variety of independent training schemes for print journalists. It accredits courses at universities and colleges and should be the first point of contact for those who need to know more about how to start on a career. Since its inception the NCTJ's short course department has provided over 500 open courses for more than 7,000 journalists. Courses are run at Bournemouth, Cardiff, Darlington, Edinburgh, Farnham, Glasgow, Gloucester, Hamilton, Harlow, Harrow, Leicester, Liverpool, Pontypool, Portsmouth, Preston, Redruth, Sheffield, Southend, Wolverhampton, Wrexham and at three centres in London.

More than 800 trainees, over half of them graduates, enter the NCTJ training scheme each year. Among the many topics on their curriculum are relevant aspects of law: contempt, libel, privilege and the complexities of the Official Secrets Act. Do you know what libel is? Most of us think we do, and when asked would say libel is written and slander is spoken, both being the offence of writing or saying scurrilous or untrue statements about someone else. In truth, that is only half the correct answer. It is just this distinction between thinking we know and really knowing that is so important. 'Libel is a statement concerning any person which exposes him to hatred, ridicule or contempt, or which causes him to be shunned or avoided, or which has a tendency to injure him in his office, profession or trade' (Fraser on *Libel and Slander*, 7th edition). For journalists a simple definition is this: libel exists when someone's character or livelihood is damaged by statements in a paper. That the allegations are true may not be adequate defence, nor that the story was published in good faith and without malice or understanding. So be careful. The legal meaning of contempt of court is also taught but this probably concerns editors and reporters more than freelance writers.

The Official Secrets Act was passed in 1989 to replace its predecessor of 1911. It makes it an offence for anyone working for the Crown to disclose, by word of mouth or in writing, information acquired as a result of their employment. This restriction applies equally to civil servants, diplomats, soldiers, policemen, members of the judiciary and even Crown gardeners, cleaners, porters and secretaries. The Act was clarified many years ago to cover matters calling for special secrecy for reasons of national security and covered the press. These restrictions were known as D Notices which were, in effect, government bans on editorial publication of specific items.

Those aged between 24 and 30 who find direct entry on to a paper the only route into journalism will not be indentured as trainees but will be registered with the NCTJ. If you start above the age of 30 you will not be registered at all, so it is important to see your training is adequate. Here the National Union of Journalists may provide invaluable assistance.

Completing a course cannot guarantee you a job on a paper or even that you will regularly turn out acceptable copy (although you should be able to by then) but you will have taken several important steps up the ladder. Some local education authorities or newspaper groups sponsor students in their college year, meeting all or part of the cost of the pre-entry course. There is a wide range of courses accredited by the NCTJ, which also supports the National Vocational Qualifications (NVQ). These are awarded by the Royal Society of Arts Examinations Board (Progress House, Westwood Way, Coventry CV4 8HS *tel* (01203) 470033 *fax* (01203) 468080) and provide formal guarantees of ability in place of apprenticeships. The NVQ aims to raise the level of proficiency among trainees and lays down standards required to turn them into competent regional journalists. Defined points of attainment comprise making routine enquiries and originating ideas, planning and carrying out assignments, writing, presenting and filing copy, and accuracy in shorthand to a standard of 100 words per minute.

If you are starting in your middle years or later and want occasional or regular work as an 'out of the office' freelance, don't consider any lack of training a disadvantage. Determination is one of the more desirable qualities in journalism, and this will be your greatest asset, whatever your age. The NUJ runs courses for freelances, both newcomers and established journalists, and will supply further information on request. Freelances who have been staff journalists might claim the skills they learned and the contacts they established give them a head start, but fortunately the passing years endow us all, if only we let them, with an unbeatable native sense, a firm spirit of application to the task and all the opportunity we could possibly wish for. Self-employed writers work in news agencies, public relations, on magazines and in broadcasting as well as on newspapers. When you really want to do it, nothing will stop you.

The National Extension College will provide expert tutors giving invaluable advice in developing ideas, targeting markets and broadening your experience as a writer. It was established in 1963 as a forerunner of the Open University and now offers over 150 courses in a variety of topics. Further details of home study courses are available from the NEC (18 Brooklands Avenue, Cambridge CB2 2HN *tel* (01223) 316644 *fax* (01223) 313586).

For postgraduate studies the University College of St Martin in Lancaster offers a three-year part-time course leading to an MA in Writing Studies. Writing can be developed within a framework that is academic and practical, in an environment both stimulating and supportive. The course is contained in ten modules and further details may be obtained from the Academic Registrar, University College of St Martin, Lancaster LA1 3JD *tel* (01524) 384384 *fax* (01524) 384385.

If you contemplate a course of training, be sure it is what you expect and hope it will be. In the arts business, as in many others, training is sometimes led by sharks. In 1996 a former postman from London was sent to prison after being found guilty of running a fraudulent so-called 'writing school'. He had netted almost £10,000 by claiming to have won international awards in the teaching of writing, that he had a contract for publishing his umpteenth novel from a major publishing house and that he was ideally experienced to teach the craft of writing. Prospective students had paid some £1,500 each before this particular shark was unmasked. There are many similar 'schools' or 'colleges'. So be wary – and remember the only safeguard you have against such people is your own caution and common sense.

Regardless of your age, there are several working aids you will find worth their weight in copy; if you haven't yet acquired them and nobody is likely to teach them to you, I strongly advise the do-it-yourself approach. The most valuable aid is shorthand, which is still irreplaceable despite all developments in modern technology. The few weeks or months it might take you to learn shorthand will be among the best-spent in your journalist training.

Can you type at speed? If you can't, teach yourself from any reputable manual or a software program. It's not difficult to learn and when you've mastered it you'll get through five times as much work as you did with the old two-finger 'Where's the apostrophe got to?' method. Shorthand and being able to work despite any amount of surrounding noise and conversation are two of the most useful and practical aids to writing I've ever learned.

The following are invaluable guides for trainees regardless of age and background:

1 *Careers in Journalism* (available from the NUJ on 0171-278 7916)
2 *Essential Law for Journalists* (Butterworths)

Rights – and wrongs

When you are employed by a newspaper, i.e. you are a full-time or part-time staff member, the copyright of everything you write for that paper is owned by its proprietor. A confusing fact is that a separate copyright exists as soon as a piece is published, and it is this that newspapers create when they print copy written by members of their staff – who are, by the nature of their contracts, barred (except in very special circumstances) from selling their 'original' copyright elsewhere. A similar restraint assigns the copyright of business writers and teachers to companies, local education authorities or other bodies, if their work is written in the course of employment by such bodies. The copyright sign ©, designed by the Universal Copyright Convention, is not required by law in the UK but is the only way to ensure protection in the 90+ countries that are parties to the Berne Convention, as we are. A study of the 1988 Copyright, Designs and Patents Act together with directives from the European Union (although in parts heavy going!) can be very revealing. For a breach of copyright to have taken place a 'substantial part' of the original work must have been copied. There is no precise definition in the Copyright Act of what is meant by 'substantial part', and when such problems have arisen in court an objective assessment of the position is made in each case. Copyright is an expression of your intellectual property; there are few assets so valuable to a freelance and its value should never be underestimated.

If you are writing as a freelance contributor, the copyright of what you have written remains in your hands (except in circumstances so rare we may almost forget about them), and when you offer your work to a paper you are merely offering the first British serial rights, i.e. your permission for the paper to be the first to print and publish your copy in this country. This being well understood and taken to be so by default, it is neither customary nor necessary to write 'First British Serial Rights' on copy sent to newspapers. It is also an understood part of the deal that a newspaper, which may be published in several editions at the same time, has the right to use work accepted from freelances in more than one edition, this being, in effect, 'one' usage only.

So what about this 'separate' copyright the paper owns once it has bought your work? While the literal contents of the written piece remain with the author, it is this separate copyright covering its exact typographical layout that is now owned by the newspaper. Is it, then, free to use it again later or sell it to someone else? In theory, yes, but only *in the exact typographical format in which it first appeared*. Knowing the established rules and practice about copyright should set minds at rest, but it cannot, alas, be claimed that all papers stick strictly to them; indeed one or two newspaper groups make no secret of assuming you are giving them all rights.

It's happening on every hand. Most national papers are now varying the rights they buy in order to allow them to reproduce material on the Internet World Wide Web – commonly referred to as the 'web'. So easy is it to reproduce on the web copy already bought and paid for (once), and so hard is it for the original writer of the copy to detect when this is being done, that the Internet is almost a spectator event, with lifting free for all. A leading jazz writer browsing on the Internet was astonished and disturbed to happen upon several pages of her book on a well-known saxophonist, without any reference to her or her publisher. She complained, and sought retraction and subsequent acknowledgement of her research and the years of hard work she had expended on the book. She threatened legal action if the publisher didn't comply and demanded a share of any royalties coming his way. With firmness, persistence and the law on her side, she won.

Countless stories are told among working journalists of sharp practice on the part of newspapers and newspaper proprietors in sending out contracts to contributors containing terms and conditions, followed by bold text saying something like 'If you agree to the above offers of engagement you do not need to sign and return this contract. A payment cheque accompanies this contract. Encashment of the cheque will constitute your acceptance of the above offer of engagement on the terms and conditions stated above.' Such wording is unenforceable in law. The 1872 Bills of Exchange Act specifically bars the use of a cheque for any purpose other than for the payment of money. It cannot be used as part of a contract and certainly not as part of any deal assigning copyright.

You might be facing this ominous (and unlawful) statement on a cheque requiring that you should sign agreement perhaps weeks or even months after the piece has been bought and published. Some ultra-cautious folk return the cheque to the paper, asking for it to be amended; they might receive an apology for the 'error', or they might hear nothing and not even get the cheque back without a battle. In fact no such correspondence is needed, for the answer is simple: cross through the claim firmly and present the cheque to the bank as usual. If there is any trouble about it from the paper in future, which is unlikely, you may have to remind them they are acting illegally and cannot take what you have not offered, any more than I can take the whole cake if you only offer me a slice.

Some newspapers try to persuade freelance writers to give up all rights for no extra pay, with the hint that if they don't agree their work may be less readily acceptable in future. Although the law confers various rights on writers we may, of course, waive those rights if we wish or are persuaded to do so. My advice about such a suggestion or request from a publisher, should you receive one, is *don't sign away all rights*; both principle and practice are at risk of being compromised.

It is not only text that is at risk. A Manchester freelance photographer sold a picture to the *Sun* after selling it to the *Manchester Evening News*, his regular employer. The next day it appeared in the *Daily Mirror*, the *Daily Express*, the *Daily Mail* and the *Daily Telegraph*. All had taken it from the *Manchester Evening News* and his exclusive deal with the *Sun* collapsed. Following his strong protest the photographer received offers of small fees for second rights from the papers who had stolen the picture in the first place.

Retouching of pix is also now so commonplace that it almost seems unretouched pix are not worth printing. Retouching so greatly improves quality it cannot be wholly condemned. But retouching with intent to deceive – that is another question. The NUJ has taken steps to see doctored pix are always identified as such. In October 1995 photographer Crispin Rodwell took legal action concerning the misuse of his original shot of a boy throwing a ball at a wall bearing the graffiti 'Time for Peace'. Without his knowledge or permission this slogan was changed to 'Recipes for Peace' for a cookery book cover to be sold in aid of a children's charity and then doctored again for a Sky TV advertising hoarding with some additional words boasting that Sky TV announced the IRA ceasefire before anyone else did so.

In 1996 the NUJ joined forces with the Authors' Licensing and Collecting Society (ALCS). The result is freelances have a chance of being properly rewarded for the reuse of their work; the same year ALCS paid out a total of £8.9 million to 15,000 members and associates. The smallest payment was £10 and the largest £24,000.

Written contracts are seldom offered to freelances nowadays, and generally the terms for each job have to be separately negotiated in the light of its (and your) value to the paper. When I began working for the *Sun* at its launch in 1959, a contract was confirmation of intent to serve by one side and security of employment by the other. Clauses dealt with the matter of rights, among other things, agreeing to the normal provisions then obtaining; the writer retained the copyright, licensing it to the paper (a daily) to be released after a period of fourteen days. In my case this meant I handed over copyright of everything I wrote for the paper for just a fortnight, after which it reverted to me to use elsewhere and in whatever manner I wished. (I may say that a daily column accumulates an enormous amount of copy over a long period and I have, with the copyright in my sole hands, been able to make extensive and profitable use of it ever since.)

You could never meet a more agreeable and friendly gathering of people than you are likely to find at seminars and conferences (few groups of potential rivals are so willing to share their trade secrets), but it is naive to imagine there aren't a few baddies seeking the easy way into their ranks. Those who lack the ability to write for themselves are not above stealing what has already been written by other people. It is increasingly difficult to spot if and when your copy is stolen by an idle so-called writer who hopes neither you nor anyone else will notice the theft.

Remember, other people may only borrow the substance, not the words. If your copy has already appeared in a newspaper you have some protection from the paper itself, although it may be hard to identify and prove any suspected theft. Naturally the reverse applies, and you must be careful not to infringe the copyright of others. The Newspaper Licensing Agency (Lonsdale Gate, Lonsdale Gardens, Tunbridge Wells, Kent TN1 1NL *tel* (01892) 360333 *fax* (01892) 525275) represents the copyright interests of virtually all national titles. It covers photocopying as well as copyright matters and is more kindly disposed to those approaching it openly than to those it subsequently finds have infringed copyright.

What is considered 'fair dealing' is bounded by a thin line unwittingly crossed by the unwary. It is fair to make a single copy of someone else's work for purposes of private study and this may extend to copying a couple of pages from a reference book. Copying a large section means trouble. But the definition of 'large' in this context remains unclear. Imagine you are reporting a speech made by a leading public figure and need to quote his exact words in your newspaper report. Written drafts of many such speeches are handed round to the waiting press before they're delivered on a platform. You are quite free to reproduce his exact words as he says them, but what if you also (then or on another occasion) copy his words from the press handout? By common consent this is allowable as long as your quote from the written speech copies it only to a reasonable extent. Again, what is reasonable? How long is a piece of string? Nobody can tell you the precise answer, but I keep my pieces of string short enough to be entirely safe. It's easy to do this; there are a dozen ways of breaking up potentially dangerous quotes or passages. In fact if you're reporting the words of politicians and others used to the sound of their own voices in public, you may well be doing the rest of us a service by lightening the text, without losing any of its meaning.

A final word on this topic: copyright lies in the expression of ideas, not in the ideas themselves. But don't spread your best ideas about too liberally. Other people may flood the market with their interpretations of your ideas before you get round to writing about them yourself – and when you do you may find the freshness has evaporated.

Being paid*

What you are going to be paid should be at the front of your mind when you are thinking about aspects of setting yourself up in business. It is a question, perhaps more than any other, so tangled and giving rise to so wide a range of opinions that few freelances can agree on the answer, while many deny there can be one.

In my experience such imprecision is just what editors like, and as long as it persists they see no reasons for clarifying the position. Put yourself in their shoes; most are no stingier than the rest of us, but the less it costs to run their papers the greater favour they're likely to find from their owners or proprietors. Naturally they don't want to be expected, let alone forced, to pay more than the low rates some can get away with now.

It's sad to hear of freelance writers so pleased to have their work accepted at all that they'll gratefully accept whatever fee is offered; some don't even know what they're going to be given until they receive it or some document reveals how much it's going to be. Can you imagine a worker in any other occupation being content with such a loose and unsatisfactory arrangement? Do you believe the newsprint suppliers, the van drivers, the secretarial staff and all the other people employed in the running of a newspaper don't know their rates of pay? Would managements or editors dream of treating them as so many of them treat freelances? Regular staff writers, please note, have a structured and recognised scale of salaries; they wouldn't put up with the treatment frequently meted out to freelances. The labour force essential to make a newspaper work depends on writers as much as it does on other workers in the industry. Managements must, of course, secure the services of staff journalists by paying them at a regular and mutually agreed rate. Freelances are lower down the scale, you say, and therefore can't expect to be treated as decently? Well, if you're resigned to being thought of as a second-class writer and don't mind being trampled on . . .

*As I write these are some of the latest figures of payment per thousand words available to me: see how they compare with yours . . .

Independent on Sunday	£400	*The Scotsman*	£140
Guardian	£200	*The Times* (supplement)	£400
Daily Telegraph	£400	*Mail on Sunday* (page lead)	£600

The usual (and some claim unalterable) method of paying freelance writers is virtually unknown in any other field. Shall I accept a coat, for instance, that a local market stallholder proffers, take it home without paying for it, hang it up in the wardrobe for a few weeks, months or even years – and then casually mention to the stallholder that I don't want it and he can have it back? Pity it's got a bit dirty and crumpled since falling on the floor and a couple of buttons are missing, but that doesn't matter, does it? Shall I try doing that and see what happens? It's not the same? I can't see the difference. When I speculatively offer a piece of work to an editor, I am like the stallholder offering that coat. The potential purchaser either wants it and is prepared to pay for it, or doesn't want it and hands it back immediately. Why should it be acceptable for an editor, a potential purchaser of manuscripts, to behave in so cavalier a fashion?

The sticky matter of getting editors to pay up when a piece has been published is a thorn in the side of most freelances at one time or another in their writing careers. More often it is the accounts department or the management rather than the editor who is the baddie on these occasions. Too often, when all else has failed, I have had to warn of legal action to follow – and several times I have been obliged to take it. It is simple and not wildly expensive, even if the case is lost. County Courts offer a 'small claims' service for the attempted recovery of debts under about £3,000 and it is best to proceed thus:

- Be confident you have a clear solid case without ambiguities or inconsistencies and that the paper you intend to sue has not gone out of business or been absorbed into another company which is not legally obliged to honour your defendant's debts. There is nothing to be gained from flogging a dead horse.

- Over a period of (say) a month, send four weekly invoices by recorded delivery, marking them 'First', 'Second' as appropriate, being sure to write this on the invoice as well as the envelope with each posting.

- After this time with no satisfaction send the final invoice stating that unless payment is received within X days, that is by (here quote a date), action will be commenced in the County Court to recover the debt.

If that doesn't work (and it often does), obtain from the court a copy of the leaflet *How Do I Make a Small Claim in the County Court?* You will also need a copy of the County Court summons (N1) – in fact it might be a good idea to pick up several so you have some in reserve to strengthen your resolve on future occasions.

- Make your claim in simple terms, giving all the facts of the case:

  My claim is against *XYZ Times*, the defendant, who published my 1,000-word article on 16 June 1998, and who have not paid the agreed fee of £195 despite repeated requests that they should do so. Interest at 5 per cent on the fee (now delayed for more than six months) amounts to a further £9.75, making my total claim £204.75.

- Sign and date the form, enclose a cheque for the court fee (calculated according to the size of the claim and ascertainable from the court office) which is payable by the loser, and send it to your local County Court.

Most bad payers then pay up. If one defends the case the proceedings will normally be transferred to his local court. That could be a long way away, so you should ask for travel and out-of-pocket expenses. Normally the settling of the case is itself informal, with you, the defendant or someone speaking on his behalf, any witnesses and the arbitrator together in a small room: no bewigged judges or complex legal formalities. Statements are made by both parties, questions posed and answered – and the decision is made. Often the whole affair lasts less than half an hour.

Once you have won the case, the court will make an order on the defendant to pay within a stated time, usually a fortnight or a month hence. And when you have the settlement cheque in your hot little hands, take note of the defendant's account number before paying it into yours. If it bounces, you can have his account frozen until it clears. Justice isn't all on the side of the baddies. One other small point: should you lose or fail to receive the money even after winning – put it down to experience. And recoup any losses by writing about it for the benefit of others who may one day find themselves in a similar situation.

Professionals take their stories to higher bidders as well as or instead of the small provincial papers. I do urge writers not to sell their work for a pittance. I realise some may be writing as freelances in their retirement, as an extra interest while fully employed in another job or because they enjoy writing but really do not need the money (and of course there is nothing wrong with any of those circumstances in themselves), but the 'I'm not bothered about the fees' brigade don't understand how much harder they are making life for their fellow writers, and even for themselves. Amateurs are fine. I've never know a writer who didn't start as one, myself included. But editors know perpetual amateurs don't expect much and that is why they don't get it.

Many freelances are writing full-time with mouths to feed and mortgages to pay. As long as editors (or whoever fixes rates of pay) can find writers willing to work for little or nothing, that's all they need offer. Perhaps the hardest lesson for beginning writers to learn (and, I regret to say, some of those willing to take 'anything' in the cause of getting published are not still beginners) is *do not undercut your worth or your colleagues by accepting less than professional fees.* Hold out for a fair return for your work. Provided you have shown an editor you can offer thoroughly professional copy he really wants, when he wants it, he won't turn you away. And afterwards he'll not only respect you but know you can be relied on to do another good job next time. The world can be hard and freelance writing is not easy; be a wimp and you'll be treated like one; be competent and diligent and you'll find plenty of work at fair rates.

NUJ rates of pay

Many freelances are unaware that there is an official list of what is considered 'fair' payment by various newspapers and magazines. The National Union of Journalists issue their freelance members with an annual guide, from which the following are extracts. I stress that all the figures quoted are basic rates from which negotiations should start:

- National dailies, i.e. all daily and Sunday titles distributed thoughout the UK, plus *The European*, the Glasgow-based *Herald*, *Daily Record* and *Sunday Mail*, Edinburgh's *The Scotsman* and *Scotland on Sunday* and the London *Evening Standard*:

    Features: very variable rates are paid depending on company policy, how desperately the paper wants the copy and (sadly) how little the freelance will accept. Broadsheets may offer less than £200 per thousand words (this rate is considered unacceptable) but fees over £300 are usual and most titles pay more, some a good deal more. Tabloids nearly always pay higher rates and are generally more willing to negotiate fees.

News: usually paid per thousand words with £200 or *pro rata* the minimum acceptable. Many papers pay more, again depending on the value of the news copy at the time. Exclusive leading stories can command large fees and one appearing as a page lead should attract £500 regardless of length.

- Regional and provincial papers, including morning dailies covering large areas, such as the *Yorkshire Post* and the *Western Daily Press*:

  Features: weeklies usually pay per line (traditionally counted as four words) at £1.85 up to and including 10 lines, with 19p for additional lines an absolute minimum. This low rate will increase dramatically according to the value of the copy and the circulation of the title. Dailies, evenings and Sundays in this category pay at least £3.24 for up to and including 10 lines, and 32p for additional lines.

  News: the recommended minimum rate for weeklies is £1.70 for up to and including 10 lines, with 17p for additional lines. For dailies, evenings and Sundays, £2.90 for up to and including 10 lines, with 29p for additional lines.

National and provincial newspapers have special rates for unusual copy such as cartoons and crosswords which are seldom accepted on an *ad hoc* basis. Negotiations for a running series in these and similar fields may begin at about £100 for a single column black and white cartoon in a national paper with about £60 for provincials; for crosswords in nationals, between £130 and £150 according to size and title circulation (and at least £300 for extra large puzzles) with a minimum of £30 from regional and provincial papers.

Rates of pay are usually defined in terms of the number of words written. But view this with caution: the paper may interpret this as payment for words published, which may not be the same thing. And some papers pay varying fees for copy published in different parts of the paper. In September 1996, for instance, the *Manchester Evening News* was paying £89.97 per thousand words for women's features and £130 for some others, with features appearing towards the back of the paper earning less than those nearer the front. No wonder writers were complaining that if the latter practice were to continue the sports writers, traditionally featured in the back pages on most days, would get nothing at all!

Remember those NUJ freelances who earn their livelihood by doing nothing else but writing. Could they, as well as non-NUJ freelances in greater numbers, survive from writing alone if there were not a properly negotiated structure of payment? It is true that not every paper, high and low, subscribes to these agreed rates, but the majority do, with the smaller ones usually belonging to greater parent groups who do. I stress that poor quality work cannot expect to receive much reward, for it is probably not worth much, but next time you're offered derisory rates for a first-class job, will you have the courage to ask for a fair rate? If the answer to such a request is a shrug indicating that's what the rate is, take it or leave it, will you just sigh and take it? Many are the arguments way into the night among journalists on this tricky point. Realistically, say some, we have to take what is offered or we don't get the work. Not so, say others, perhaps those who can more easily afford to pick and choose. Every time we accept poor pay, they insist, we are hammering another nail in our own coffins. On this matter you must make up your own mind.

Where do you fit in?

'But I am not a member of the National Union of Journalists,' you may be saying, 'so do the rates quoted above apply to me, and am I entitled to expect to receive them?'

How much to accept, or to charge if asked to quote a rate for a particular job, is one of the thorniest issues facing a freelance writer. On the whole it is best to use the NUJ rates as a guide, so at least you know where to start thinking about the rewards for your work. You should also be prepared to be flexible until you're sufficiently well known for editors to come looking for you (yes, that may take some *years*) instead of your courting them. At all stages of your writing career you must be ready to negotiate fees, and this should always be done before writing the relevant copy. You may spend nine or ten hours on one piece and earn £150, or you may toil at research and writing another for five hours and earn £750. Only you can be the judge of where and how to price yourself at the right level for each job without selling yourself short. Believe me, this tricky task becomes easier with long-term practice and familiarisation with the markets.

If you regularly sell to local papers, particularly any not part of a larger group, or to a locally produced publication, you may begin to perceive a pattern of fees, depending on the nature of the publication and the company producing it. Your normal market study of the readership, advertising and general viability will guide you as to whether you are receiving a fair and reasonable return for your work.

Plagiarism

The infringement of copyright, whether others do it to you or you do it to them, and regardless of whether it is deliberate or innocent, is called plagiarism. The history of literature is riddled with it, from the time an Ancient Egyptian scribe found temporary fame by 'lifting' the words an earlier sage had written on the sides of a pillaged tomb, to the alleged plagiarism of a well-known Roald Dahl story and parts of Margaret Mitchell's *Gone with the Wind*. (Lawyers and inborn newspapermen/women among you may notice how instinctively the word 'alleged' stuck itself in there; omitting that important adjective, and thereby implying an accused is guilty before it has been proved so, has caused many a writer and newspaper horrible trouble.) Inexperience and immaturity are no excuse: in 1996 a 15-year-old Somerset schoolboy won the Hansard's Young Political Writer of the Year award with his story on the then Tory MP Michael Portillo. Alas, the story was directly copied from a feature in the *Economist* written by David Lipsey. Bang went the 15-year-old's reputation as well as his £500 prize. In cases where big-selling works are said to have been victims of plagiarism (there's that caution again), huge sums of money may be awarded in compensation if they are proved, but in smaller cases which some folk may think hardly worth bothering about, the principle remains. Plagiarism is theft, and there's no refuting that.

The mere reporting of what seem to be straightforward facts can be surprisingly risky; research will often take different researchers down the same paths because they are the logical and reasonable paths to follow. How do you deal with raw facts and figures? Write that Josiah Blogsworth invented sandpaper in Harrogate in 1623 (I do hope he didn't because I think I've just invented him) and will you be guilty of plagiarism because a book you consulted in your research said he did? Hardly, any more than you could be in trouble for mentioning rain is wet and cats can't read. Plagiarism is a complex matter but it doesn't deal in nonsense. Like copyright, it needs to be studied and have its awesomeness appreciated before being stored (for all time, we hope) under the bed.

Jargon

Since you began reading this book you have heard a lot of jargon. All occupations have their own, much of it originating long ago and referring to working practices now out of date. It is not surprising that by the very nature of their business those whose work is words enjoy a particularly rich store of jargon. Here is some that will soon be familiar to you:

agency copy material coming from a major news agency
ampersand '&', the typographical sign for 'and'
banner the main headline across the top of the page
blink the act of connecting to networking communication
body type the size of type used for most of the paper
bold thick dark type used for emphasis
byline a writer's name at the head of a story
caps capital letters
casting off ending a story, generally in a given space
catchline an identifying phrase/word at the top of a page
copy any matter to be set in type
copy-taster the person assigned the task of assessing copy
crosshead or shoulder a subheading, often in bold type, to enliven text
draft a temporary or unfinished story
ear the advertising space beside front page title-line
edition a one-time print (perhaps with regional variations)
embargo a ban on publication until a specific time
file to submit copy for publication
freebie a gift or privilege from a reader/advertiser
fudge box space for late news; also an item in a ruled box
house style spelling, punctuation, etc. as the paper likes it

intro the opening paragraph
layout sheet ruled into columns showing where copy will go
lead the main news story in the paper
lift to pass off someone else's work as your own
literal a printing error in spelling, ect. (*sic*)
lower case small (not capital) letters
masthead heading on editorial page giving details of paper
NIBS small items of news, 'news in brief' pars
par a paragraph
point a standard unit of type size; also means a full-stop
proofs the first print for checking before the final print
run on where a story is not to be broken into pars
slush a pile of unsolicited and often unwanted copy
spike an imaginary or actual spike for rejected copy
standfirst an intro separate from the story itself
story a written item or piece of work
streamer a page lead printed across several columns
stringer writer (usually overseas) always ready to file copy
splash a page one lead story
strap a subsidiary headline above a main headline
shorts small stories for fillers or down-page items
tag the small type line after the main headline
tabloid a page half the size of a broadsheet
tear sheet a page carrying published copy
upper case capital letters
widow a word alone on a line

In a lifetime of writing I have met and made friends with many hundreds, perhaps thousands, of writers and I've never found one who was not an optimist; privately, very often, and sometimes without admitting to it or being aware of it, that quiet unshakeable optimism is the deepest support at the back of the mind when success seems far away. Writing is an easily abandoned occupation and to make the grade takes determination and staying power. Somewhere buried among those characteristics is the most important of all – an involuntary compulsion. Nobody forces you to do it, as there are countless other ways of keeping the bills at bay, but a compulsion to write means you must. I count it a fortunate handicap (if it may even be called so), for writing is also a way of making money.

Finale

'It must be true,' said an acquaintance, 'I read it in the paper.'

Such assumption of the integrity of the press made me both happy and sad; happy to hear the speaker's confidence in high standards, yet sad to know all newspapers sometimes fall short of them. Given that the aim of all journalists is to be read and that the market is fiercely competitive, the temptation to embroider, exaggerate and distort newspaper copy is considerable. Exciting and revealing stories about people in the public eye are always *interesting*, and papers founded with the intention of printing only good news have short lives. Too often we read of reporters harrassing victims of crime or misfortune, while biased, ill-informed and factually distorted copy appears in print somewhere every day; the power of the press is not always used wisely.

In every case there are arguments on both sides; it is difficult to decide where the boundaries lie between the exposure of fraud or evil, in the interest of the general public, and the preservation of privacy. The practice of newspapers paying witnesses in criminal trials, for instance, is a problem. Banning such payment would be a restriction on freedom of speech, says one lobby, claiming payments are justified because papers couldn't get the stories without paying important witnesses. Opponents argue that paying witnesses is for commercial gain to get 'exclusivity' and increase sales, which itself denies rival papers freedom of speech. So is paying witnesses a charter for freedom or a proper business practice?

The official view of the Press Complaints Commission is that payment or offers of payment for stories, pictures or information should not be made to witnesses or potential witnesses in current criminal proceedings or to people engaged in crime or other associates (including family, friends, neighbours and colleagues) except where the material concerned ought to be published in the public interest and the payment is necessary for this to be done.

The public interest would include

- Detecting or exposing crime or serious misdemeanour
- Detecting or exposing anti-social conduct
- Protecting public health and safety
- Preventing the public from being misled by some statement or action of that individual or organisation
- Payments should not be made either directly or indirectly through agents

Journalists do not enjoy a good image. What can we do – what can *you* do – to improve our reputation? Being in a position to write about other people imposes on us a moral responsibility to tell the truth as it appears to us. That means not only in news reports or when dealing with facts and figures, but also in the way we represent people, their circumstances and their lives. We must never belittle them or write anything to make them look foolish or less worthy than we find them. Just as speech may be given variety of meaning with accompanying raised eyebrows or a mock severity, so what we write may be carelessly (or, alas, deliberately) laden with innuendo: the journalistic sneer, the glib approach, the suave assertions made over innocent people's heads. Such insinuation cheapens journalism because it is writing with less than honesty. If we want the public to trust us we must first show ourselves to be trustworthy.

Many freelances never do better than work hard with no pension, no sick pay, no expense accounts, free stationery or perks, no paid holidays or any contractual continuity or security. Yet failure always was the mother of success, and success is a journey rather than a destination. So it is a curious paradox that the results of success can be difficult to bear.

Newspaper journalists are ready to take knocks and very soon become used to them. No matter how much you try not to upset anyone or what pains you have taken not to offend any of your likely readers, it is inevitable that one day someone somewhere will take exception to something you've written. If the error is due to sub-editing your first thought might be to get an apology printed to absolve yourself from blame. This is easier said than done for it may seem as if the people you hoped would be 'on your side' are the very ones to scupper your chances. No paper wants to print an acknowledgement that it made a mistake in an earlier edition. Getting one to print an apology or retraction may be impossible, except under legal pressure – and then you can be sure the amendment will be as small and insignificantly placed as possible.

A line has been omitted from your copy, or two lines have been transposed, making nonsense of one of the sentences that gave you most satisfaction? Your scrupulous punctuation has gone to pot with an outbreak of unwanted apostrophes, a couple of pars have been inverted and the final line rounding your copy off so neatly is missing altogether? What aggravation, and what should you do about it? You'd be foolish to go storming off to the editor, or to any of his underlings. Like every journalist I've had my share of irritations and I expect there are more in the pipeline for me just waiting for stories I haven't yet written. When something goes wrong, a deep breath and a private sigh at the inefficiencies of everyone but you are all you may allow yourself. Just take care the next mistake isn't yours, for without constant alertness we all succumb to complacency and carelessness. Meeting the challenge of continual disappointment with a strong determination to succeed will certainly prove any writer's ability. But stubborn persistence is not enough; banging your head against a brick wall will, eventually, only wear down your head. Finding another way of breaking down the wall is the solution; that's the professional way. And it's amazing that the more professional you are, the more editors need you.

Be a freelance journalist and you shoulder a responsibility that will keep you on your toes. When the ink gets into your veins, there's no job to beat it.

'Put it to them briefly so they will read it, clearly so they will appreciate it, picturesquely so they will remember it and, above all, accurately so they will be guided by its light.' (Joseph Pulitzer, 1847–1911, American newspaper owner and editor who established the Pulitzer Prizes)

Index

163

cable channels 32
Caedmon 58
Caesar, Julius 84
calls 8, 12
Capital Gains Tax 136
Careers in Journalism 145
Caribbean Times 30
cartoons 46, 154
casting off 75
catchlines 113
Caxton 14
CD-ROMs 100
Chambers Dates 100
Chambers Dictionary 101
Chambers Idioms 100
Chartered Institute of Journalists 106
Chaucer 58
chequebook journalism 20
children 10
China Daily 32
cinema 24, 60
Citizens' Advice Bureau 12, 137
Civil War 121
clarity 62, 65, 67, 70
clichés 64
colleges *see* training
*Collins Electronic English
    Dictionary & Thesaurus* 101
colour supplements 26, 37
come-ons 2, 72
comic strips 46
commas 65, 73–74
Commentaries 84
communications 31
compact discs 100
complaints 94–95
    letters 77
    see also Press Complaints
        Commission
compositors 14–15
Conan Doyle, Arthur 80
Concise Dictionary of Confusables
    99
Concise Oxford Dictionary 101
*Concise Oxford Dictionary of
    English Etymology* 99
*Concise Oxford Dictionary of
    Proverbs* 99
*Concise Oxford Dictionary of
    Quotations* 99
conferences
    editorial 6, 12
    writers' 107–108, 148

contempt 14, 20, 142
contracts 144–148
cookery 10, 148
copyright 2, 145–149, 156–157
Copyright, Designs and Patents Act
    145
copytakers 50, 123–124
copy-tasters 14, 37
Correct English 99
correspondents 11, 33, 36, 110, 121
Courier & Advertiser 30
courts 12, 14, 145
    County 151–152
    reports 141
cover prices 16, 23, 26, 121
crossheads 13, 113
crosswords 8, 10, 53, 154
Customs & Excise 137
cut-offs 2, 75–76

D Notices 143
Dahl, Roald 156
Daily Courant 121
Daily Deshbarata 31
Daily Express 18, 28, 32, 147
Daily Herald 18
Daily Mail 18, 28, 55, 121, 147
Daily Mail and General Trust 32, 141
Daily Mirror 18, 28, 32, 121, 147
Daily News 24
Daily Record 30, 32, 153
Daily Star 28, 32
Daily Telegraph 28, 32, 121, 141,
    147, 150
Daily Universal Register 121
dashes 70
deadlines 52–53
density 66–67
depreciation 136
Dewey Decimal system 103
diary 10, 42
Dickens, Charles 18, 102
Digital Future 116
Directory of Writers' Circles 107
distribution 5–6, 17, 24
diurnals 120
double spacing 112
drafts 61, 68, 91
drama 54
dummy 5

Economist 156
electronic mail 110